CW00525011

THE NEWEST AIR FRYER COOKBOOK

1500 Days Amazing & Delicious Air Fryer Recipes for Everyday Enjoyment

TABLE OF CONTENTS

POULTRY RECIPES 38

DESSERTS RECIPES 51

BREAKFAST & BRUNCH RECIPES 64

SALADS & SIDE DISHES RECIPES 75

VEGETABLE & & VEGETARIAN RECIPES 81

INTRODUCTION

An air fryer is a kitchen appliance that allows you to cook foods with hot air instead of oil. It's like having your mini convection oven on your countertop! Air fryers rapidly circulate hot air around the food inside the basket or tray. This creates a crispy exterior while locking in moisture and flavor inside. Unlike deep frying or baking in oil, there's no need for excess oils or fats when using an air fryer, making it a healthier cooking option overall. Using my air fryer has become second nature now that I understand its functionality. With adjustable temperature controls and various settings, including pre-programmed modes for specific foods like chicken wings or French fries – cooking with my air fryer feels effortless and foolproof. Plus, it cooks frozen foods well, and fresh veggies are given a new life thanks to this nifty appliance!

BENEFITS OF USING AN AIR FRYER FOR COOKING CANNED FOODS

HEALTHIER COOKING METHOD

I love using my air fryer for cooking canned foods because it's healthier than deep-frying. Using hot air instead of oil makes the food crispy without adding unnecessary calories and fat. This technique also helps retain more nutrients, making it an excellent option for those who want to eat healthily. I don't have to worry about that greasy feeling after eating fried foods. Air frying canned vegetables like green beans or baked goods like biscuits can be a tasty way to enjoy them without all the added fats from traditional frying methods. For example, when I air fry canned green beans with some seasoning and a touch of oil spray, they come out perfectly crispy on the outside and tender on the inside – just what I'm looking for in a side dish! It's amazing how such simple changes can make our meals healthier while tasting delicious. Overall, using an air fryer as an alternative cooking method is perfect for those who want to cut back on oily or fatty foods but still enjoy satisfying snacks and meals. Learning how to cook canned foods in my air fryer has been fun and rewarding as someone who loves experimenting with different recipes and ingredients.

TIME-SAVING

Using an air fryer to cook canned foods is not only healthier but also a time-saving method.
You can have your favorite canned foods cooked in just minutes with the right temperature and timing settings. Compared to traditional cooking methods such as baking or frying, an air fryer reduces cooking time by about 20-30%. It saves cooking time, and cleanup is faster and easier with an air fryer. Unlike conventional ovens or stovetops that require multiple pots and pans, air fryers typically have one removable basket that's easy to clean. Plus, they don't produce much smoke or odor during cooking, making them ideal for quick meals on busy days.

VERSATILITY IN COOKING DIFFERENT TYPES OF CANNED FOODS

One of the most significant benefits of air frying canned foods is its versatility in cooking different canned foods. You can cook almost anything in a can using an air fryer, from vegetables and meats to baked goods, seafood, snacks, and appetizers. For example, canned green beans are a popular vegetable easily cooked in an air fryer for a healthier alternative to traditional fried green beans. And if you're looking for something more substantial, try making honey-barbecue chicken wings or spicy tuna cakes using your air fryer. The possibilities are endless when it comes to cooking canned foods in an air fryer. With so many options available, knowing which canned foods work best for air frying and how to prepare them properly before placing them inside the appliance is essential. With these tips and tricks under your belt, you'll be on your way to creating delicious meals with ease!

REDUCED OIL USAGE

One of the most significant benefits of cooking canned foods in an air fryer is the reduced use of oil. Unlike traditional frying methods, you only need a fraction of the oil to achieve crispy and delicious results. This makes it a healthier alternative for those conscious of their calorie intake. With less oil usage, air frying also minimizes the risk of ingesting harmful substances in heated oils. Compared to deep-frying or sautéing, air frying allows you to cook your favorite canned foods with minimal added fats without compromising taste and texture. By choosing the suitable types of canned foods and coating them lightly with seasoning or batter, you'll have a guilt-free pleasure that will satisfy your cravings without sacrificing your health goals.

CHOOSING THE BEST CANNED FOODS FOR AIR FRYING
When choosing canned foods to air fry, consider the types of vegetables, meats, baked goods, seafood, and snacks that can be fried with reduced oil usage and increased crispiness.

VEGETABLES---I love air frying vegetables because they are healthier and deliver crispy and delicious results. My favorite canned vegetables to cook in the air fryer are green beans and corn, but you can use almost any vegetable you have on hand. Just remember to drain excess liquid before coating them with seasoning or batter. One crucial tip for air frying veggies is not to overcrowd the basket. This ensures that each piece gets evenly cooked and crispy. I also recommend setting the temperature between 375-400°F and cooking for 8-12 minutes, depending on your desired level of crispiness. And if you want an added flavor, try tossing your veggies in a bit of melted butter or oil mixed with herbs or spices before adding them to the basket!

MEATS---Meats can be a delicious addition to your air fryer repertoire. Some great canned meat options include chicken, beef, and pork. Before cooking, drain any excess liquid from the can and pat dry with paper towels. When preparing canned meats for air frying, you can coat them in various seasonings or batter for added flavor and texture. Remember that wet batter should be avoided as it will not cook evenly in the air fryer. Instead, use a dry coating or spices like paprika or garlic powder. By following these tips and experimenting with different recipes, you'll soon discover how versatile your air fryer can be when cooking canned meats!

BAKED GOODS---Baked goods are a delicious addition to any meal and can be made even better using an air fryer. Canned biscuits, cinnamon rolls, and gingerbread bites are just a few examples of baked goods that can be made in the air fryer. The reduced oil usage makes them healthier and creates a crispy outer layer. When preparing canned baked goods for air frying, it's important to coat them with seasoning or batter before cooking. This will help enhance their flavor and create an even crispier texture. Wet batter foods should not be placed in the air fryer since they tend to cook unevenly, while corn dogs should be pre-fried before being air fried for best results. Following these tips and tricks, you can enjoy perfectly cooked canned baked goods straight from your trusty air fryer!

SEAFOOD---I love cooking seafood in my air fryer. It's a healthier alternative to deep frying and cooks the fish to a perfect crisp. My favorite canned seafood to air fry include shrimp, crab cakes, and even tuna patties. Before you air fry your seafood, drain any excess liquid from the can and season it with your preferred spices or batter for extra flavor. Set your air fryer temperature between 350-400 degrees Fahrenheit, depending on the type of fish you're cooking, and cook them for about 5-8 minutes per side until they are crispy on the outside and tender on the inside. Remember not to overcrowd your air fryer basket, which can cause uneven cooking or lead to food sticking together. With these simple tips, you'll be able to enjoy perfectly cooked canned seafood every time!

SNACKS AND APPETIZERS---Don't forget about snacks and appetizers when it comes to air-frying canned foods. Air fryers can create deliciously crispy and healthier versions of favorite crunchy snacks like popcorn or kale chips. For a heartier snack or party appetizer, try air-frying frozen meatballs or chicken wings for a quick cook time and crispy texture. Remember that wet batter foods should be avoided in the air fryer, but a light coating of seasoning or breadcrumbs can add extra flavor to your snack creations. Another great option for snacking is air-fried sweet potato fries. Sweet potatoes are an excellent source of vitamins A and C and are perfect for those seeking a healthier alternative to traditional french fries. Slice the sweet potatoes into thin strips, coat them with oil and seasoning, then pop them into the air fryer until crispy and tender. With these tasty options, your next game-day spread will be a hit!

PREPARING CANNED FOODS FOR AIR FRYING

Before air frying canned foods, it's essential to drain excess liquid from them and coat them with seasoning or batter for added flavor and texture.

Draining Excess Liquid

When preparing canned foods for air frying, one essential step is draining excess liquid. This is because too much liquid can cause steam, making your food come out soggy instead of crispy. Ensure you use a strainer or colander to drain any excess water while shaking it well to prevent dripping. For best results, it's recommended that you pat dry the canned foods with paper towels after draining off any liquids. Doing this helps remove more moisture from the food and provides a dry surface for seasoning or coating with batter. By draining excess liquid before cooking, your air-fried canned foods will come out deliciously crispy and perfectly cooked inside!

Coating With Seasoning Or Batter

When it comes to air frying canned foods, adding seasoning or batter can make a world of difference in taste and texture. Try coating vegetables like green beans or sliced potatoes with breadcrumbs mixed with your favorite spices for crispy results. Mix cinnamon and sugar and dredge slices of canned pineapple before placing them in the air fryer for a sweeter option. However, it's important to note that wet batter should not be used when cooking canned foods in an air fryer. The high heat from the appliance will cause the batter to blow around inside the basket and cook unevenly. Instead, opt for dry coatings like panko breadcrumbs or crushed cornflakes for that perfect crunch without making a mess.

Setting Up Your Air Fryer For Cooking Canned Foods

To ensure your canned foods are cooked to perfection in your air fryer, it's vital to set up the appliance correctly – this includes selecting the right temperature and time settings and preheating the basket. Read on for more tips and tricks on making the most out of your air fryer when cooking canned foods!

Temperature And Time Settings

When it comes to air frying canned foods, setting the right temperature and time is crucial for a successful outcome. It's always best to refer to the manual that came with your air fryer for guidance. Generally, most air fryers have a temperature range between 200-400°F, and cooking times can vary between 5-25 minutes depending on your cooking. Preheating your air fryer beforehand is also essential, ensuring even cooking and better results. Once preheated, adjust the temperature settings and watch the food cook. It's always helpful to shake or flip your food halfway through cooking time for an evenly cooked result. Remember, every dish has unique temperature requirements, so consult recipe instructions before starting.

Preheating The Air Fryer

Preheating your air fryer ensures that your canned foods cook evenly and crisp. To preheat your air fryer, set the temperature to the recommended level and allow it to heat up for a few minutes before adding your food. It's important not to overcrowd the basket during this process as it can affect the cooking time. Once preheated, place your canned foods in the basket and set the timer according to the recipe or instructions on the packaging. Remember to check on your food halfway through cooking, using tongs or a spatula to flip them over for even cooking. By taking these steps and following our helpful tips, you'll be able to achieve deliciously crispy canned foods cooked in an air fryer every time!

CLEANING YOUR AIR FRYER PROPERLY

Cleaning your air fryer properly is crucial to maintaining its efficiency and prolonging lifespan. This includes removing excess grease and food debris, wiping down the interior and exterior of the appliance, as well as checking and replacing the air filter regularly.

Removing excess grease and food debris

I always make sure to clean my air fryer properly after each use. To remove excess grease and food debris, I use a damp cloth or sponge to wipe down the exterior and interior of the appliance. It's important to be gentle while cleaning to not damage the non-stick coating. Another helpful tip is removing leftover crumbs or debris from the bottom of the basket using a kitchen brush or toothbrush. Add dish soap and water to your cloth or sponge for extra cleaning power if there are stubborn stains. Keeping your air fryer clean and free from buildup will perform better and last longer overall.

Wiping Down the Interior And Exterior Of The Air Fryer

Keeping your air fryer clean is essential to prevent buildup and ensure optimal performance. Wiping down the interior and exterior of the air fryer is crucial in maintaining its longevity. After each use, allow the appliance to cool before unplugging it and wiping down the inside with a damp cloth. To clean the exterior of your air fryer, wipe it down with a damp cloth or sponge. Avoid using harsh chemicals or abrasive materials that could damage the surface. Regular cleaning will keep your appliance looking new and prevent any unwanted odors from forming while cooking different types of foods. Remember to also check and replace your air filter regularly per manufacturer instructions. This ensures that airflow remains consistent during cooking, resulting in evenly cooked food every time you prepare something delicious in your beloved air fryer!

Checking And Replacing The Air Filter Regularly

A critical aspect of maintaining your air fryer is regularly checking and replacing the air filter. The air filter ensures that your appliance operates properly by preventing dust and other particles from entering the heating element. Over time, the air filter can become dirty, clogged, or damaged, affecting its ability to trap debris effectively. To check the condition of your air filter, gently remove it from its slot at the back of the unit. If you notice any signs of damage or excessive buildup on the filter, it's time to replace it with a new one. Most manufacturers recommend replacing your air filter every three months for optimal performance and longevity of your appliance. By checking and replacing your air filters regularly, you'll enjoy better-tasting foods cooked in a cleaner environment while extending the lifespan of your valuable kitchen gadget.

AIR FRYERS FREQUENTLY ASKED QUESTIONS

Can I put oil in an air fryer? ----- Most recipes only call for about 1 tablespoon of oil, which is best applied with a mister. Fatty foods, like bacon, won't need you to add any oil. Leaner meats, however, will need some oiling to keep them from sticking to the pan.

What shouldn't you put in an Air Fryer? ----- The Air Fryer is one of those kitchen inventions that seem too good to be true. You can cook practically any food in the hot air multi-cooker. However, there are mistakes a lot of us do when handling an air fryer including not preheating your air fryer, not giving the air fryer enough space, overcrowding the air fryer basket, using too little oil, cutting vegetables too small, using wet batters and not washing the air fryer often enough.

Can I use Aluminum Foil or Baking Paper in the Air Fryer? ----- As a general rule, you can use both on the bottom of the air fryer if the basket sits on top. Using aluminum foil or baking paper in the basket technically can be done as long as it's weighed down by the food however it's not recommended because an air fryer works by providing a constant air flow around the cooking cavity.

Should I shake the basket while cooking? ----- Yes, shaking is allowed. A number of foods will stick to the basket if you don't shake it while cooking. Giving it a little shake is specially helpful if you overlap foods, this way the contents of the basket will cook evenly.

What's the first thing I should cook in my new Air Fryer? ----- The most common foods to start with are French Fries, and also Chicken Drumsticks.

What are the disadvantages to cooking in an Air Fryer? ----- The only real disadvantage to cooking in an air fryer is the fact most of the air fryers on the market have small cooking cavities.

What kind of foods can you cook in an Air Fryer? ----- The air fryer is your ticket to healthier fried foods that still taste crispy-crunchy delicious and leaves you with a lot less mess at clean-up time. Whether frozen food or raw meat or reheating leftover food, the hot air multi-cooker does a fantastic job. Having an air fryer means you can go ahead and cook frozen food such as frozen fries, nuggets, fish sticks etc. You can also cook raw meat, for example you can roast chicken or pork in the fryer. And you can certainly roast vegetables and nuts too and let's not forget you can easily bake small items.

Should I pause the Air Fryer when checking on the food? ----- Since you generally only spend a matter of seconds checking, or shaking the food, it is not necessary to pause the air fryer.

Can I open the Air Fryer while cooking? ----- Every Air Fryer is slightly different however going on the premise that heat rises, if your air fryer opens by sliding a basket out from the side or front, then there should be no reason why you can't open the basket for short periods of time.

Should I preheat the Air Fryer? ----- Every Air Fryer manufacturer will have their own recommendations for their particular air fryer. This is also a good idea since many users find that cooking times are more accurate if you preheat first.

Why are my cooking times different? -----Remember, not all Air Fryers are created equal. Air Fryers work by circulating hot air around the food. The internal shape of the Air Fryer and how the air flows, as well as how hot the air is all contribute to how long it takes to cook a food. This is why you should check often and only use temperatures as a guide until you know how your particular Air Fryer cooks.

What are the advantages to cooking in an Air Fryer? ----- Advantages are many, like we said before, we're talking about a healthier form of cooking. Even though your food is fried it won't be dripping with oil. It's less expensive to run. Cooking in an air fryer is very quick. Also, food cooked in an air fryer is generally really tasty simply because the food is crispy on the outside, and juicy and tender on the inside.

BEEF, PORK & LAMB RECIPES

Air Fryer Ham Steaks

Servings: 1

Cooking Time: 10 Minutes

Ingredients:

- 1 ham steak
- 2 tablespoons butter, melted
- 2 tablespoons brown sugar, packed
- 1 teaspoon honey* (optional)

Directions:

1. Preheat your air fryer to 380 degrees.
2. Remove the ham steak from its packaging.
3. Mix the brown sugar and melted butter together in a bowl.
4. Place ham steak in the air fryer and baste half of the mixture on top of the ham slice.
5. Cook for 10-12 minutes, flipping and basting the ham steak again halfway through.
6. Remove from the air fryer and drizzle optional honey on top.

Notes

add honey only if not using a honey ham

Air Fryer Brown Sugar And Honey Glazed Ham

Servings: 10

Cooking Time: 55 Minutes

Ingredients:

- 2-3 pounds (.9-1.36 kg) boneless, fully cooked ham
- BROWN SUGAR GLAZE
- 1/2 cup (110 g) brown sugar
- 1/4 cup (60 ml) honey
- 1/4 cup (60 ml) orange juice (or 1 orange juiced)
- 2 Tablespoons (60 ml) mustard (optional) or apple cider vinegar
- 1/4 teaspoon (1.25 ml) Cinnamon
- 1/4 teaspoon (1.25 ml) Clove
- black pepper , to taste
- Aluminum Foil
- 8" square Baking Pan

Directions:

1. Remove the ham from the fridge and allow to come up to room temperature, about 2 hours before cooking.
2. Make the Glaze: In a small saucepan or microwave safe bowl, combine the brown sugar & honey glaze ingredients (brown sugar, honey, orange juice, optional mustard or apple cider vinegar, cinnamon, clove, and black pepper). Heat (can be done on the stovetop or in the microwave) and whisk until brown sugar is dissolved and glaze is well combined. Set aside.
3. If the ham has a netting, remove it from the ham. If ham is not pre-sliced, score the ham with shallow 1/2-inch criss-cross cuts.
4. For Basket Style Air Fryers: Line the air fryer basket with 2 pieces of long, overlapping foil sheets (see step-by step photos on website write up above). Lay the ham on top of the foil and then brush with some of the glaze to coat the ham. Close the foil over the ham and wrap tightly.
5. For Oven Style Air Fryers: Place the ham in an 8"x8" baking pan which fits in your air fryer (you may need to trim the edges of the ham to fit your pan and air fryer size). Brush with some of the glaze and close foil over the ham, wrapping tightly.
6. Air Fry at 340°F/170°C for 25 minutes. Open the foil and brush the ham with more glaze (make sure to reserve some glaze for finishing & serving). Close the foil tightly, and Air Fry again at 340°/170°C for 25 minutes.
7. After air frying for the 50 minutes, open up the foil again and now push the foil down around the edges of the ham if using the basket-style air fryer method. Create a boat with the foil that holds the juices and keeps the ham from drying out. If using the Oven Style Air Fryer method, just remove the foil from the 8"x8" pan.

8. Brush with a little more glaze and increase heat to Air Fry at 360°F/180°C for about 5 minutes, or until caramelized to your liking.
9. Let ham rest for 5 minutes before serving.
10. Optional serving: Combine the juices from the air fryer basket and the remaining glaze in a saucepan. Bring to a simmer and cook for about 5 minutes or until thickened. Brush the glaze onto the ham when serving or serve in a bowl.

Air Fryer Chuck Roast

Servings: 6
Cooking Time: 45 Minutes

Ingredients:

- 2 pounds beef chuck roast
- 1 tablespoon olive oil
- ½ tablespoon Worcestershire sauce
- 1 ½ teaspoons kosher salt
- 1 ½ teaspoons garlic powder
- 1 teaspoon onion powder
- 1 teaspoon dried thyme
- 1 teaspoon dried rosemary
- 1 teaspoon black pepper

Directions:

1. Line the inside of your air fryer with aluminum foil. Preheat the air fryer to 390 degrees F.
2. In a small bowl, whisk together olive oil and Worcestershire sauce. In a second small bowl, combine the salt, garlic powder, onion powder, thyme, rosemary, and pepper.
3. Rub the roast with the olive oil-Worcestershire sauce mixture, then rub the herb mixture over the entire roast. Place the roast in the basket of your air fryer.
4. Air fry for 15 minutes, then carefully flip the roast. Air fry at 320 degrees F for another 45-60 minutes, depending on the size of the roast.
5. Remove, allow to rest for 10 minutes, then slice and serve with your favorite sides.

Air Fryer Steak Bites

Servings: 4
Cooking Time: 6 Minutes

Ingredients:

- 1 pound sirloin steak or strip loin or ribeye
- 1 tablespoon vegetable oil
- 1 tablespoon soy sauce
- 1 ½ teaspoons Worcestershire sauce
- 2 cloves garlic minced
- 1 tablespoon melted salted butter
- salt & pepper to taste
- 1 tablespoon fresh parsley

Directions:

1. Cut steak into 1-inch cubes. Toss with oil, soy sauce, Worcestershire sauce, garlic, salt & pepper. Marinate 15 minutes.
2. Preheat air fryer to 400°F.
3. Remove the steak bites from the marinade and dab dry. Toss with melted butter.
4. Add steak bites to the air fryer basket in a single layer and cook 6-7 minutes or until browned. Do not overcook.
5. Toss with parsley and additional butter if desired. Serve with horseradish sauce below.

Notes

Cook steak bites in batches if needed. Do not overcrowd the air fryer.

Whisk together the following for Horseradish Dipping Sauce:

¼ cup sour cream

2 tablespoons mayonnaise

1 ½ tablespoons prepared horseradish

1 teaspoon fresh lemon juice

1 small clove garlic

salt & pepper to taste

Air Fryer Bacon Cauliflower Mac And Cheese

Servings: 6

Cooking Time: 10 Minutes

Ingredients:

- 4 strips bacon
- 1 cup water
- 1 small cauliflower diced
- 4 ounces cream cheese
- ¼ cup heavy cream
- 2 cups cheddar cheese shredded
- 1 teaspoon salt
- ¼ teaspoon cayenne pepper
- 1 teaspoon paprika
- green onions or parsley finely chopped, for garnish

Directions:

1. Cook the bacon in the air fryer for 5 minutes. Dice into small pieces.
2. In a microwave-safe bowl - add one cup of water and the cauliflower. Microwave for five minutes. Check for tenderness. If still hard cook another few minutes. Drain.
3. Preheat Air Fryer to 400°F.
4. In the same bowl, combine the cream cheese, heavy cream, one cup of cheese, salt, cayenne, bacon, and paprika. Microwave one more minute.
5. Put the cauliflower mixture in a Vortex-safe dish. Place on the lowest shelf - use a quick cover if you have one to keep the top from browning too quick.
6. Cook for 4 minutes. Remove top and cook for 2 more until golden brown.

Notes

This can also be done in an Instant Pot - close lid and set for 2 minutes. Quick release. Add all of the ingredients and close the lid and manual cook for one more minute. Quick-release. Enjoy!

Air Fryer Meatball Sub

Servings: 4

Ingredients:

- 2 large eggs
- 2 tsp. balsamic vinegar
- Kosher salt and pepper
- 1/3 c. panko
- 4 large cloves garlic (2 grated and 2 chopped)
- 1/4 c. freshly grated Parmesan cheese, plus more for serving
- 1/2 c. flat-leaf parsley, chopped
- 8 oz. sweet Italian sausage, casings removed
- 8 oz. ground beef
- 1 lb. cherry tomatoes
- 1 red chile, sliced
- 1 tbsp. olive oil
- 4 small hero rolls, split and toasted
- 6 tbsp. ricotta cheese
- Basil, for serving

Directions:

1. In a large bowl, whisk together eggs, vinegar and 1/2 teaspoon each salt and pepper. Stir in panko and let sit 1 minute. Stir in grated garlic and Parmesan, then parsley. Add sausage and beef and gently mix to combine.
2. Shape meat mixture into 20 balls (about 1 1/2 inches each) and place in a single layer on air-fryer rack (the balls can touch but should not be stacked; cook in batches if necessary). Air-fry meatballs at 400F for 5 minutes.
3. In a bowl, toss tomatoes, chile and chopped garlic with oil and 1/4 teaspoon each salt and pepper. Scatter over meatballs and continue air-frying until meatballs are cooked through, 5 to 6 minutes more.
4. Spread ricotta on toasted rolls, then top with meatballs, grated Parmesan, roasted tomatoes and chile and basil if desired.

Air Fryer Herb Crusted Roast Beef

Servings: 6

Cooking Time: 1 Hour 20 Minutes

Ingredients:

- 1.2 kg piece beef scotch fillet
- 1 tablespoon olive oil
- 2/3 cup (80g) panko breadcrumbs
- ¼ cup (20g) finely grated parmesan
- 2 tablespoon chopped flat-leaf parsley
- 1 tablespoon chopped tarragon
- ¼ cup chopped chives
- 2 cloves garlic, crushed
- ¼ cup (70g) wholegrain mustard
- 1 teaspoon smoked paprika
- olive oil cooking spray
- 150 grams swiss brown mushrooms, halved (or quartered if large)
- 150 grams button mushrooms, halved (or quartered if large)
- ¾ cup (180ml) thickened cream
- to serve: roast potatoes

Directions:

1. Preheat a 7-litre air fryer to 200°C/400°F for 5 minutes.
2. Brush beef with 2 teaspoons of the the oil and season.
3. Taking care, place beef in the air fryer basket; at 200°C/400°F, cook for 15 minutes, turning halfway through cooking time, until browned all over.
4. Meanwhile, combine the breadcrumbs, parmesan, parsley, tarragon, half the chives and half the garlic in a bowl, then season. Transfer beef to a plate and pat dry with paper towel. Working quickly, spread 2 tablespoons of the mustard over the top and sides of the beef, sprinkle with paprika, then firmly press on breadcrumb mixture. Spray breadcrumbs generously with cooking spray.
5. Return beef to the air fryer basket, then cover basket tightly with foil. Reset the temperature to 180°C/350°F; cook for 30 minutes. Remove foil.
6. Toss mushrooms in remaining oil and add to the air fryer basket with beef; cook, without foil, for a further 10 minutes until beef is medium or cooked to your liking (see testing meat when ready to right) and mushrooms are browned. Transfer beef to a dish; cover loosely with foil and rest for 15 minutes.
7. Meanwhile, to make creamy mushrooms, combine cream and remaining garlic and mustard in a medium saucepan over medium heat; add the mushrooms and any
8. cooking juices from the bottom of the air fryer pan and bring to the boil. Reduce heat; simmer, stirring occasionally, for 5 minutes or until sauce thickens slightly.
9. Stir in remaining chives and season to taste.
10. Thinly slice beef and serve with creamy mushrooms and roast potatoes.testing meat when readyInsert a meat thermometer into the thickest part of the beef. The internal temperature should reach:
11. rare 55–60°C/130–140°F
12. medium–rare 60–65°C/140–150°F
13. medium 65–70°C/150–160°F
14. medium–well done 70–75°C/160–170°F
15. well done 75°C/170°F

Air Fryer Beef Empanadas

Servings: 8

Cooking Time: 16 Minutes

Ingredients:

- 8 Goya empanada discs (in frozen section, thawed)
- 1 cup picadillo
- 1 egg white (whisked)
- 1 teaspoon water

Directions:

1. Spray the air fryer basket generously with olive oil spray to avoid sticking, or line the basket with air fryer parchment paper.
2. Place 2 tablespoons of the picadillo in the center of each disc. Fold in half and use a fork to seal the edges. Repeat with the remaining dough.
3. Whisk the egg whites with water, then brush the tops of the empanadas.

4. Air fry in a single layer, in batches as needed 350F 8 minutes, turning halfway or until golden. Remove from heat and repeat with the remaining empanadas.

Notes

How to Bake Empanadas in the Oven: If you don't have an air fryer, you can also bake them in the oven at 400 degrees on a nonstick baking sheet for about 18 to 20 minutes until golden.

How to Freeze Empanadas: You can flash freeze the uncooked empanadas on a sheet pan. Once frozen, transfer to a freezer-safe container for up to 3 months.

Air Fry From Frozen: Pop the frozen empanadas right into your air fryer and air fry 350F for about 12 minutes, turning halfway until golden and hot.

Air Fryer Steak

Servings: 4

Cooking Time: 12 Minutes

Ingredients:

- 4 8-oz Top sirloin steaks (at least 1 inch thick, preferably 1.5 inches; other high-quality steaks with similar thickness will also work)
- 2 tsp Sea salt
- 1/2 tsp Black pepper
- 1/2 recipe Compound butter (optional)

Directions:

1. Remove your steak from the fridge about 30 minutes before cooking to bring it to room temperature. (This will ensure even cooking.)
2. Make compound butter according to the instructions here. Refrigerate until ready to serve.
3. Preheat the air fryer to 400 degrees F (204 degrees C).
4. Pat the steaks dry with paper towels. Season the steaks liberally with sea salt and black pepper on both sides.
5. Arrange the steaks in the air fryer in a single layer, so the pieces are not touching or only minimally touching (cook in batches if needed; don't crowd the basket). Air fry until the steaks reach your desired doneness (use a probe thermometer for best results). For 1.5-inch thick steaks, that's about 10-12 minutes for rare, 11-13 minutes for medium rare, 12-14 minutes for medium, 13-15 minutes for medium well, or 14-16 minutes for well done. Use a meat thermometer to check for the right temperature – 120 degrees F (52 degrees C) for rare, 130 degrees F (54 degrees C) for medium rare, 140 degrees F (60 degrees C) for medium, 150 degrees F (66 degrees C) for medium well, or 160 degrees F (71 degrees C) for well done. The temperature will rise by another 5 degrees F while resting (see next step).

6. Remove the steaks from the air and transfer to a plate. Top each with 1 tablespoon (14g) of compound butter.
7. Let the steaks rest for 5 minutes before slicing against the grain.

Air Fryer Crispy Chilli Beef Recipe

Ingredients:

- For the crispy beef
- 450g Beef Strips
- 4 tbsp Cornflour
- 2 tsp Sesame Oil
- 1 tsp Chinese 5 Spice
- 1 tsp Chilli Powder
- ½ tsp Salt
- ½ tsp Black Pepper
- For the sauce
- 200ml Beef Stock
- 4 tbsp Rice Wine Vinegar
- 2 tbsp Sweet Chilli Sauce
- 2 tbsp Sesame Oil
- 1 tbsp Soy Sauce
- 1 tbsp Tomato Puree
- 1 tbsp Honey
- 1 tsp Ginger
- 2 Cloves Garlic, Crushed
- 2 Spring Onions, Chopped
- 1 Red Chilli, Chopped
- 1 Red Pepper, Sliced

- 1 Green Pepper, Sliced

Directions:

1. Add the cornflour, Chinese 5 spice, black pepper, salt, and chili powder to a bowl and stir together.
2. Add beef strips to the bowl and ensure they are fully coated in cornflour mixture.
3. Drizzle 1 tsp of sesame oil at the bottom of the air fryer and add the beef strips in a single layer. Top with another tsp of sesame oil.
4. Cook the beef strips in the air fryer for 10 minutes at 200°C until crispy.
5. Meanwhile, add together the soy sauce, tomato puree, sweet chili, honey, rice wine vinegar, beef stock, and 1 tbsp of sesame oil and stir thoroughly. Set aside.
6. Heat up 1 tbsp of sesame oil in a frying pan and add the crushed garlic and chopped red chilli and stir together.
7. Add the 2 chopped spring onions, sliced red pepper and sliced green pepper to the pan, then add your mixed together sauce and stir through all the vegetables and cook this on high heat until the sauce has thickened.
8. Finally, add the crispy beef and coat it in the sauce.
9. When everything is coated and cooked, serve with egg noodles or rice and top with fresh chilies, spring onions, and sesame seeds.

Air Fryer Bacon

Servings: 2

Cooking Time: 10 Minutes

Ingredients:

- 3 strips of bacon any thickness

Directions:

1. First, preheat the air fryer to 350°F.
2. Next, slice each strip of bacon in half and lay them on your air fryer pan next to each other. They can be overlapping a little bit, but not all the way.
3. Air fry bacon at 350°F for: thin bacon: 6-7 minutes, medium bacon: 8 minutes, or thick bacon: 9-10 minutes. Flip bacon halfway through the bake time. If you like your bacon crispy, continue cooking for

an extra 30 seconds to 1.5 minutes depending on the thickness of your bacon.

Tips & Notes

If you are planning to cook multiple rounds of bacon, make sure to discard excess grease that will build up on the bottom of your air fryer pan. This is to prevent smoking.

Make sure to keep an eye on your bacon as it can burn easily. The 350°F temperature should help prevent smoking, so don't cook your bacon any higher than that. Speaking from experience :D

Air Fryer Gingery Pork Meatballs

Servings: 4

Ingredients:

- FOR NOODLES
- 6 oz. rice noodles
- 1/2 c. Asian-style sesame dressing
- 1 large carrot, shaved with julienne peeler or cut into matchsticks
- 1/2 English cucumber, shaved with julienne peeler or cut into matchsticks
- 1 scallion, thinly sliced
- 1/4 c. cilantro, chopped
- FOR MEATBALLS
- 1 large egg
- 2 tsp. grated lime zest plus 2 Tbsp lime juice
- 1 1/2 tbsp. honey
- 1 tsp. fish sauce
- Kosher salt
- 1/2 c. panko
- 1 cloves garlic, grated
- 2 scallions, finely chopped
- 1 tbsp. grated fresh ginger
- 1 small jalape?o, seeds removed, finely chopped
- 1 lb. ground pork
- 1/4 c. cilantro, chopped

Directions:

1. Prepare noodles: Cook noodles per package directions. Rinse under cold water to cool, drain

well and transfer to large bowl. Toss with dressing, carrot, cucumber and scallion; set aside.

2. Prepare meatballs: In large bowl, whisk together egg, lime zest and lime juice, honey, fish sauce and ? teaspoon salt; stir in panko and let sit 1 minute. Stir in garlic, scallions, ginger and jalape?o, then add pork and cilantro and mix to combine.

3. Shape into Tbsp-size balls and air-fry at 400F (in batches, if necessary; balls can touch but should not be stacked), shaking basket occasionally, until browned and cooked through, 8 to 12 minutes. Fold cilantro into noodles and serve with meatballs.

Air Fryer Steak Fries

Servings: 4
Cooking Time: 12 Minutes

Ingredients:
- Frozen Air Fryer Steak Fries:
- 1 bag Frozen Steak Fries
- Homemade Air Fryer Steak Fries:
- 4 Russet Potatoes
- 1 tbsp olive oil
- 1 tsp salt

Directions:
1. Frozen Steak Fries
2. For frozen steak fries, arrange the fries in the basket, without stacking or overlapping.
3. Cook the fries at 400 degrees F for 12 minutes. Shake the basket halfway through cooking. Depending on the air fryer, the actual cooking time may vary.
4. Homemade Steak Fries
5. Peel, rinse, and cut 4 medium Russet Potatoes into straight strips.
6. In a large bowl, soak the potato strips in cold water, for about 30 minutes. Drain, and pat the fries dry.
7. Toss the fries in 1-2 tbsp of olive oil, and then season with salt, or other desired seasonings.
8. Cook at 400 degrees F for 20-25 minutes, shaking the basket halfway through cooking, until golden and crispy. Serve warm with your favorite toppings.

Air Fryer Roast Pork Belly

Servings: 1
Cooking Time: 1 Hour

Ingredients:
- 2 teaspoons fennel seeds
- 2 teaspoons sea salt flakes
- 2 teaspoons dried chilli flakes
- 2 teaspoons finely grated lemon rind
- 2 teaspoons cloves garlic, crushed
- 1 teaspoon olive oil
- 1 kilograms piece boneless pork belly, rind scored
- to serve: extra sea salt flakes, roast potatoes and roast shallots

Directions:
1. Preheat a 7-litre air fryer to 180°C/350°F for 3 minutes.
2. Place fennel seeds, salt and chilli flakes in a mortar and pestle; crush lightly. Add lemon rind, garlic and oil; pound to combine. Pat pork belly rind dry with paper towel. Rub fennel mixture all over pork.
3. Taking care, place pork, skin-side up, in the air fryer basket. Reset the temperature to 200°C/400°F; cook for 25 minutes until skin crackles.
4. Reset the temperature to 160°C/325°F; cook pork for a further 25 minutes until tender or an internal temperature of 70°C–75°C/158°F–167°F is reached on a meat thermometer. (If pork is overbrowning, cover with foil.)
5. Thickly slice pork and sprinkle with extra salt flakes; serve with any cooking juices from the bottom of the air fryer pan, roast potatoes and roast shallots.

Air Fryer Short Ribs

Servings: 2-4
Cooking Time: 15 Minutes

Ingredients:
- 1 pound short ribs (pork or beef), 1.5-inch pieces
- 1 tablespoon vegetable oil
- 1 tablespoon soy sauce (or oyster sauce)
- 1 tablespoon Shaoxing wine (optional)

- 1/2 teaspoon salt
- 1/2 teaspoon ground black pepper
- 1/2 teaspoon garlic powder
- 1/2 teaspoon paprika
- 1/4 teaspoon ground cumin powder
- 1/4 teaspoon crushed red pepper (optional)
- 1 teaspoon cornstarch

Directions:

1. In a large mixing bowl or Ziploc bag, combine the ribs with all the ingredients and mix well to coat evenly. If you use the Ziploc bag, press the seasoning around to coat evenly. Let the marinated ribs rest for at least 15 minutes to soak in all the flavour.
2. Place the marinated ribs in a single layer in the air fryer basket. Cook at 350F for 13-15 minutes until golden brown and crispy. Shake the basket halfway to cook the ribs evenly. (See recipe tips for oven bake and deep fry instructions).
3. Serve immediately with your favorite dipping sauce, such as spicy mayo, sweet chili sauce, ketchup, or ranch.

Notes

How to bake in the oven: Place the marinated short ribs in a single layer on a parchment-lined quarter sheet baking pan and bake at 400F for 15-20 minutes until crispy and golden brown.

How to deep fry: Heat oil in a medium cooking pot (at least 2-inches deep) over medium high heat for 3-4 minutes until the oil shimmers. Deep fry the marinated ribs until golden brown, about 5-7 minutes. Turn the ribs occasionally to get an even golden crust on all sides. Transfer the ribs on a paper towel lined plate to drain excess oil.

How to store: Keep air fryer short ribs in an airtight container in the fridge for up to 3-4 days.

How to reheat: Reheat these dry short ribs in the air fryer at 350F for 5 to 10 minutes until warm and crispy. You can also reheat them in a 350F preheated oven for 10 to 15 minutes.

Air Fryer Flank Steak

Servings: 4

Cooking Time: 15 Minutes

Ingredients:

- 1 pound flank steak
- 1 teaspoon Kosher salt
- 1/2 teaspoon ground black pepper
- 1 teaspoon garlic powder
- 1 teaspoon paprika

Directions:

1. Place steak in a shallow cooking dish once removed from the refrigerator to reach room temperature, for about 20-30 minutes before cooking. This helps the meat cook more evenly and ensures a tender steak.
2. Next make the rub for flank steak in medium mixing bowl. Combine the salt, pepper, garlic powder, and paprika.
3. Use paper towels to pat the steak dry.
4. Cover the steaks with saran wrap or place them inside an unsealed storage bag.
5. Use a meat tenderizer and gently pound the steak to break down the connective tissues and make the meat tender.
6. Gently rub the seasoning mix on both sides of the steak.
7. Spray the basket with oil, this will help crisp up the top and bottom of the steak.
8. Place the steak in the prepared air fryer basket and cook at 350 degrees F for 8 minutes, flipping the steak halfway through the cooking process.
9. Check the internal temperature of the steak with a meat thermometer.
10. Once the steak has reached 130 degrees F, (which brings the steak to a medium doneness) remove it from the basket or add 2-3 minutes cook time for a more well-done steak.
11. Place the cooked steak on a cutting board, cover it with foil, and allow flank steak rest time for at least 5 minutes so juices can redistribute, and steak remains juicy.

12. Slice flank steak against the grain with a sharp knife for maximum tenderness.
13. Move juicy flank steak to platter and serve.

Notes

Because it is important to eat properly cooked meat, the surest and safest way to determine doneness, is with a meat thermometer. According to the FDA, proper temperatures for steak doneness, are:

Rare-125 degrees F

Medium Rare-135 degrees F

Medium-145 degrees F

Medium Well-155 degrees F

Well Done-160 degrees F

Optional Favorite Dipping Sauces: Creamy basil sauce, red wine sauce, steak sauce, creamed horseradish, red wine vinegar with sour cream, peppercorn sauce or cheesy garlic sauce.

Optional Additional Toppings: Fresh parsley, sauteed green bell pepper, slices of heirloom tomato mixture, cotija cheese, fresh cilantro leaves or grilled chopped pineapple.

Air Fryer Candied Bacon

Servings: 4

Cooking Time: 10 Minutes

Ingredients:

- 1 pound bacon
- ¼ cup brown sugar

Directions:

1. Place bacon slices in a shallow dish with brown sugar. Toss bacon slices well so both sides are coated with brown sugar.
2. Place slices in the air fryer basket, working in batches so they don't overlap while air frying.
3. Air fry at 380 degrees F for 10-12 minutes until bacon is crispy. Remove slices and place on a cooling rack or on a plate to cool before eating.

Notes

No matter if you call this millionaire bacon or billionaire bacon, everyone will agree that this pig candy is yummy! I like to use dark brown sugar for this recipe as it makes it a delicious treat.

Cooking the bacon in the air fryer is also a great way to keep the bacon grease separate from the bacon, as it will fall through the bottom of the air fryer basket.

But did you know that you can actually use that leftover bacon grease for other air fryer recipes and cooking recipes? I'll save it and store it in a jar and then use it for cooking at other times. (It's really good to use when you're popping popcorn!)

Air Fryer Bacon Wrapped Brussel Sprouts

Servings: 4

Cooking Time: 13 Minutes

Ingredients:

- 8 slices bacon regular and sliced in half
- 16 small Brussels sprouts
- ¼ cup brown sugar

Directions:

1. Wrap one slice of halved bacon around each brussels sprout, seal with a toothpick if necessary. Repeat until all sprouts have been wrapped.
2. In a large glass bowl, toss wrapped sprouts with brown sugar, until they are well coated.
3. Place in the air fryer basket, without stacking or overlapping.
4. Air Fry at 380 degrees F for 13-16 minutes, until bacon is crispy.

Notes

Variations

Change up the flavor of bacon - You can use salty bacon, crispy bacon, thick cut bacon, or any piece of bacon or strip of bacon that you want. Maple bacon sounds like some pretty good strips of bacon to add to this easy recipe!

Add toppings - Let's be truthful here and say that toppings are always a crowd-pleaser. Drizzling some olive oil with salt and black pepper on top of this delicious appetizer adds taste in an easy way.

You can add soy sauce to these tender brussels sprouts after they are done cooking, or add some sweetness with a drizzle of maple syrup!

Air Fryer Taco Ring

Servings: 6

Cooking Time: 6 Minutes

Ingredients:

- 1/2 pound lean ground beef
- 1/4 cup water
- 2 tablespoons taco seasoning mix
- 1 cup shredded cheddar cheese
- 1 can crescent rolls

Directions:

1. In a medium skillet, cook ground beef on medium to high heat until meat is completely browned.
2. Remove from heat and drain excess grease out of the skillet. Add water and taco seasoning, stirring to coat meat. Add any additional taco ring mix-ins, such as jalapeños or onions.
3. Line the air fryer basket with a piece of parchment paper.
4. Open the can of crescent rolls, separate each roll and then lay out rolls on the parchment paper, so they are slightly overlapping at larger ends of the triangles to form a round sun shape.
5. Evenly spoon the ground beef around the center of the crescent roll circle. Then top beef with cheese, along with optional fillings such as onions or jalapenos.
6. Next lift the tops of each crescent roll over the beef mixture, and tuck under the circle, so it is sealed, and mixture will not come out.
7. Air fry at 350 degrees F for 6-8 minutes until dough has completed the cooking process and is golden brown.
8. Carefully lift the taco ring out of the basket and serve individual taco crescents while hot.

Notes

Optional Favorite Toppings: Diced green onions, ripe olives, refried beans, queso cheese, chopped tomato, crispy tortilla chips, sweet corn, shredded lettuce, black beans or salsa.

Optional Favorite Dipping Sauce: Hot sauce, bit of nacho cheese, garlic aioli, sour cream, guacamole or salsa Verde.

Substitutions: Monterey jack, ground chicken, a cheese stick, Mexican cheese, ground turkey or cream cheese.

Air Fryer Country Style Ribs

Servings: 5

Cooking Time: 20 Minutes

Ingredients:

- 2 lbs ribs country-style
- 1 tsp smoked paprika
- 1 1/2 tsp garlic powder
- 2 tsp ground black pepper
- 5 oz barbecue sauce

Directions:

1. Rinse the ribs and then pat them dry. Add the garlic powder, smoked paprika, and ground black seasoning to a small bowl and set aside.
2. Preheat the air fryer to 380 degrees Fahrenheit. Prepare the basket of the air fryer with nonstick cooking spray.
3. Rub the ribs with a small amount of the seasoning mixture.
4. Place the ribs in a single layer in the basket of the air fryer. Cook at 380 degrees for 20 minutes. Remove the basket and brush barbecue sauce onto the tops and sides of the ribs. Place back into the air fryer and cook for an additional 2 minutes. Check the internal temperature with a meat thermometer to ensure the pork has reached 145 degrees Fahrenheit.
5. Serve with your favorite sides.

Notes

Store leftover country-style ribs in an airtight container in the refrigerator for up to 3 days.

This recipe was made using a Cosori 1700 watt 5.8 qt basket style air fryer. All air fryers can cook differently. It's always best to test a small batch before cooking the entire meal to decide if our air fryer requires more or less time.

Air Fryer Bbq Chops

Ingredients:

- 500g chops washed and cleaned, pat dry
- 1 teaspoon crushed garlic
- 1/2 teaspoon crushed green chilli
- 1/2 teaspoon salt
- 1/2 teaspoon onion powder
- 1/2 teaspoon garlic powder
- 1/4 cup spare rib marinade
- 1/4 cup BBQ sauce

Directions:

1. Marinate chops in above ingredients, allow to marinate overnight. In drawer 1 add in your chops, set the air fryer on air-fry, 180 degrees celsius for 20 minutes. On turn food prompt baste chops with left over marinate.
2. In drawer 2, place your pre-cooked garlic bread, air-fry for 2 minutes on 180 degrees celsius, to melt butter and bread to soften. And then press the synch finish button. This feature allows both drawers to finish cooking at the same time.
3. Serve immediately with all your favourite braai sides, enjoy.

Air Fryer Boneless Pork Chops

Servings: 2 - 2

Ingredients:

- 2 8 oz boneless pork chops (1.25" thick)
- Kosher salt and freshly ground black pepper
- 2 tsp. pork rub (optional)

Directions:

1. Set air fryer to 400F and preheat 3 to 4 minutes. Pat pork chops dry, and season both sides with salt and pepper and/or a spice rub.
2. Place pork chops into heated air fryer and cook, 6 minutes.
3. Flip chops and cook until internal temperature on an instant read thermometer reads 135F-145F, 5-8 minutes. If it's not warm enough, continue cooking, checking every 2-3 minutes, until cooked through.

4. Cover chops with a tent of aluminum foil and let rest 5 minutes, to allow chops to reabsorb juices, before slicing and eating.

Air Fryer Grilled Ham And Cheese

Servings: 4
Cooking Time: 7 Minutes

Ingredients:

- 2 tablespoons mayonnaise
- 8 slices white bread
- 2 tablespoons Dijon mustard
- 8 slices deli ham
- 4 large slices Swiss cheese
- 8 dill pickle slices
- cooking spray

Directions:

1. Spread mayonnaise on one side of each slice of bread. With mayo side down, lightly spread 4 slices of bread with Dijon mustard, evenly top each with Swiss cheese, ham slices, folded to fit, and pickle slices. Place the remaining 4 bread slices on the sandwiches, mayo side up, and lightly press sandwiches to close.
2. Preheat the air fryer to 380 degrees F (193 degrees C). Spray the air fryer basket with cooking spray or line with a parchment liner.
3. Place sandwiches in the air fryer basket in a single layer, leaving some space around them. You may have to cook the sandwiches in batches, depending on the size of your fryer.
4. Cook until sandwiches begin to brown, 3 to 4 minutes. Flip, and cook until cheese has melted and sandwiches are golden brown, 2 to 3 minutes more. Slice sandwiches in half and serve warm.
5. Note:
6. Mayonnaise is the only thing I use these days on grilled sandwiches. It's always ready, spreads easily, browns beautifully, and has no mayo flavor. But you can use butter, if you prefer. Air fryer cooking times may vary depending on the brand and size. So watch your sandwiches closely, especially toward the end of cooking.

SANDWICHES & BURGERS RECIPES

Keto Friendly Game Day Burgers

Ingredients:

- Mini Beef Burgers:
- 1.5 pounds ground beef
- 1/4 cup onion, diced
- 1 tsp salt
- 1/4 tsp pepper
- 1 tsp brown Mustard
- Low Carb Sauce:
- 1/2 cup mayonnaise
- 1 tsp white wine vinegar
- 1 tsp paprika
- 1 tsp garlic powder
- 1 tsp onion powder
- 4 tbsp dill pickle relish

Directions:

1. Using your hands mix together the beef, onion, salt, pepper, and brown sugar (optional.)
2. Form into 15-20 mini balls.
3. Cook in your air fryer, flipping half way to your desired doneness, 7-8 minutes at 390 degrees.
4. While the burgers are cooking, mix your mayonnaise, white vinegar, paprika, garlic powder, onion powder, and dill pickle relish together. Set to the side.
5. Place each burger on a skewer with cheese, lettuce, pickles, and the special sauce.
6. Enjoy!

Air Fryer Hamburgers

Servings: 4
Cooking Time: 8 Minutes

Ingredients:

- 1-pound ground beef, thawed (preferably 80/20)
- 1 clove garlic, minced
- 1/2 teaspoon salt
- 1/4 teaspoon pepper

Directions:

1. Preheat air fryer to 360 degrees.
2. Mix together the ground beef, minced garlic, salt, and pepper with your hands.
3. Form ground beef into 4 patties and press them down with the back of a pie plate to make them evenly flat.
4. Place hamburgers in a single layer inside the air fryer.
5. Cook for 8-12 minutes, flipping halfway through cooking for medium-well hamburgers.*
6. Carefully remove hamburgers from the air fryer,** place onto hamburger buns (if using), and add desired toppings.

Notes

thicker hamburgers may take longer to cook if not pressed down properly

if making cheeseburgers, place a piece of cheese on each burger in the air fryer, turn the air fryer off, and let the burgers sit in the air fryer for 1 to 2 minutes until melted

Air Fried Crispy Chicken Sandwiches

Servings: 4

Ingredients:

- 2 large chicken breasts, cut in half and pounded to an even thickness
- 1 cup buttermilk
- 1 tablespoon kosher salt or 1 teaspoon table salt
- ¾ cup panko breadcrumbs
- ½ cup all-purpose flour
- ½ teaspoon salt
- ¼ teaspoon dried oregano
- ½ teaspoon paprika
- ¼ teaspoon garlic powder
- ¼ teaspoon dried thyme
- ¼ teaspoon ground ginger
- ½ teaspoon ground black pepper
- Oil spray

- 4 brioche burger buns
- Assorted toppings such as lettuce, tomato, onions and additional condiments

Directions:

1. Place the chicken breasts in a zipper top bag and pour in buttermilk and salt. Squeeze the air out and seal the bag. Marinate in the refrigerator for at least an hour or preferably overnight.
2. In a shallow bowl combine the panko breadcrumbs, flour and spices.
3. Remove the chicken breasts from the buttermilk. Remove excess buttermilk and dredge in the breadcrumb mixture.
4. Arrange the chicken breasts in one layer on a parchment-lined baking sheet, thoroughly coating chicken with oil spray on both sides.
5. Air Fry at 375°F for 20 – 25 minutes or until internal temperature reads 165°F and the chicken breasts are golden brown and crispy. For more even cooking, flip the chicken halfway through and spray with more oil if desired.
6. Serve chicken sandwiches on toasted brioche buns with lettuce, tomatoes, red onion and other favorite condiments.

Air Fryer Grilled Cheese Sandwich

Servings: 2
Cooking Time: 7 Minutes

Ingredients:

- 8 slices white bread
- 1 tablespoon butter
- 4 slices cheese

Directions:

1. Spread a light layer of the butter on one side of each piece of bread.
2. Place the buttered side down in the air fryer basket.
3. Cover the slice of bread with a piece of cheese. Then top the cheese with another slice of bread, with the buttered side up.
4. Air Fry at 370 degrees F for 3-5 minutes. Then flip, and air fry for 2-3 additional minutes, until bread reaches desired crispness.

Notes

Make this a heartier meal by adding a few slices of bacon to the sandwich, avocado slices, or on inside of slices, spread bread with pesto sauce before adding cheese.

Depending on the type of bread you use, you may want to adjust the cook times. For softer bread, or French Bread, air fry until it reaches your desired crispness.

Air Fryer Bacon, Egg And Cheese Biscuit Breakfast Sandwiches

Servings: 8

Ingredients:

- 1 can (16.3 oz) refrigerated Pillsbury™ Grands!™ Southern Homestyle Original Biscuits (8 Count)
- 6 eggs
- 1/4 teaspoon salt
- 1/8 teaspoon pepper, if desired
- 1 tablespoon butter
- 8 slices cooked bacon, cut in half crosswise
- 8 slices (3/4 oz each) American cheese

Directions:

1. Spray bottom of air fryer basket with cooking spray. Separate dough into 8 biscuits. Place 4 biscuits in air fryer basket, spacing apart.
2. Set air fryer to 330°F; cook 6 minutes. Using tongs or spatula, turn over each biscuit. Cook 4 to 5 minutes or until biscuits are deep golden brown and cooked through. Remove from air fryer; cover loosely with foil to keep warm while cooking second batch. Cook remaining biscuits as directed above.
3. Meanwhile, in medium bowl, beat eggs, salt and pepper thoroughly with fork or whisk until well mixed. In 10-inch skillet, heat butter over medium heat just until butter begins to sizzle. Pour egg mixture into skillet. Cook until set, stirring occasionally.
4. To serve, split warm biscuits; top bottom half of each with scrambled eggs, bacon and cheese. Cover with top halves of biscuits.

Air Fryer Frozen Burger

Servings: 2

Cooking Time: 15 Minutes

Ingredients:

* 2 frozen burger patties

Directions:

1. Place frozen burgers in a single layer in the basket of the air fryer.
2. Air fry the burgers at 350 degrees Fahrenheit for 15 minutes, flipping the burgers halfway through cook time.
3. If desired, add sliced cheese during the last minute of cooking time.
4. Carefully remove the burgers from the air fryer and serve them with your favorite toppings.

Notes

If adding cheese, top with sliced cheese during the last minute of cook time.

Serve bunless for a healthier burger.

Air Fryer Chicken Burgers

Servings: 4

Cooking Time: 10 Minutes

Ingredients:

* 1 pound ground chicken
* 1 large egg
* 1 cup mozzarella cheese shredded
* 1/2 cup onion finely chopped
* 1/2 cup panko breadcrumbs
* 1 teaspoon minced garlic
* 1/2 teaspoon kosher salt
* 1/4 teaspoon ground black pepper

Directions:

1. Preheat air fryer to 365 degrees F.
2. In a large bowl, combine the chicken, egg, cheese, onion, panko crumbs, garlic, salt and pepper. Mix chicken mixture together with your hands until fully combined.
3. Divide the chicken mixture into 4 equal parts and shape them into 5-inch diameter burgers.
4. Spray the air fryer basket with non-stick cooking spray and place the chicken patties in air fryer in a single layer.
5. Air fry the chicken burgers at 365 degrees F for 8-10 minutes or until cooked through, depending on the thickness of the patties.
6. Use a meat thermometer to confirm internal temperature of burger patties which should be a safe temperature of 165 degrees F.
7. Allow chicken burgers to cool for a couple of minutes then carefully remove them from the basket.
8. Serve while hot or let them continue to rest on a baking rack.

Notes

Optional Additional Favorite Sauces: BBQ sauce, mustard yogurt sauce, chili sauce, ketchup, spicy sriracha sauce (based on your spice level), honey mustard, marinara sauce, relish or a sweet and spicy pickle.

Optional Favorite Toppings: Shredded lettuce, slice of tomato, raw or caramelized onions, sundried tomato strips, bacon, avocado, pepper jack cheese, American cheese or shredded cheese.

Cooking Tips: Use a silicone mat to make it an easy clean up and prevent food sticking to your basket. For crispy chicken patties brush a little olive oil on the patties prior to placing them in your air fryer.

I make this recipe in my Cosori 5.8 qt. air fryer. Depending on your air fryer, size and wattages, your cooking time may need to be adjusted 1-2 minutes.

Greek Lamb Burgers With Baked Eggplant Fries

Servings: 4

Ingredients:

* Nonstick cooking spray
* 1 pound ground lamb
* 2 ounces feta cheese, crumbled (about ½ cup)
* ½ cup grated red onion (from 1 small onion), divided
* 1 ½ tablespoon olive oil, divided

- 2 ½ teaspoons kosher salt, divided
- ¾ teaspoon freshly ground black pepper, divided
- 1 ½ cups panko
- 2 large egg whites
- 1 medium eggplant, cut into ½-by-1-by-2-in. wedges
- ½ cup grated English cucumber (from ½ cucumber)
- 1 cup plain whole-milk Greek yogurt
- 2 teaspoons fresh lemon juice (from 1 lemon)
- Hamburger buns and lettuce, for serving

Directions:

1. Preheat oven to 425°F. Lightly coat a rimmed baking sheet with cooking spray. Stir together lamb, cheese, ¼ cup onion, 1 tablespoon oil, 1 teaspoon salt, and ½ teaspoon pepper in a bowl until just combined; shape into 4 patties.
2. Combine panko and remaining 1½ teaspoons salt in a large ziplock plastic bag. Whisk egg whites in a large bowl until foamy. Dip eggplant wedges, 1 at a time, in egg whites and transfer to bag with panko. Once all eggplant has been added to bag, seal and shake well to coat. Arrange eggplant in an even layer on prepared baking sheet and coat generously with cooking spray. Bake until golden brown, about 20 minutes, flipping halfway through.
3. Meanwhile, heat remaining ½ tablespoon oil in a large nonstick skillet over medium-high. Add lamb patties and cook, flipping once, until browned, about 4 minutes per side for medium.
4. Place cucumber and remaining ¼ cup onion on a paper towel. Squeeze gently to release liquid. Transfer to a small bowl and stir in yogurt, lemon juice, and remaining ¼ teaspoon pepper.
5. Place patties on buns with lettuce and yogurt sauce. Serve with eggplant fries and remaining yogurt sauce.

Air Fryer Biscuit Egg Sandwiches

Servings: 4

Ingredients:

- Deselect All
- Nonstick cooking spray, for the molds
- 4 large eggs
- Kosher salt
- 4 thin slices deli ham
- One 16.3-ounce tube refrigerated flaky biscuit dough, such as Pillsbury
- Hot sauce, for serving

Directions:

1. Special equipment: 4 silicone baking cups, 6-quart air fryer
2. Spray 4 silicone baking cups with nonstick spray. Transfer the cups to the basket of a 6-quart air fryer.
3. Whisk together the eggs in a large glass measuring cup until no white streaks remain. Season with 1/2 teaspoon salt. Divide the eggs among the baking cups. Insert a piece of ham into each cup, crumpling it to make it fit (some of the ham should stick out above the surface of the eggs).
4. Tear off 4 biscuits from the tube of dough. Place each biscuit in the basket of the air fryer in a single layer. Set the air fryer to 300 degrees F and cook for 10 minutes. The biscuits should be golden brown; transfer to a cutting board.
5. Gently lift each egg muffin from its mold so you can see if it's set. If there's no liquid egg on the bottom, transfer the mold to the cutting board. If there is liquid egg on the bottom, cook for up to 1 minute more.
6. Slice each biscuit in half crosswise. Remove the egg muffins from the molds and slice in half crosswise. Arrange the two egg halves on each bottom biscuit, drizzle with plenty of hot sauce and sandwich with the top biscuit.

Air Fryer Burgers From Frozen Patties

Servings: 4

Cooking Time: 15 Minutes

Ingredients:

- 4 frozen raw beef patties , usually sold as either 1/4 lb.(113g) or 1/3 lb.(150g)
- salt , to taste if needed
- Lots of black pepper
- oil spray , for coating
- BURGER ASSEMBLY:
- 4 Buns , + optional cheese, pickles, lettuce, onion, tomato, avocado, cooked bacon etc.
- EQUIPMENT
- Air Fryer
- Instant Read Thermometer (optional)

Directions:

1. Spray both sides of frozen burger patties with oil. Season with salt and pepper if needed. Spray the air fryer basket with oil and place the patties in the basket in a single layer. Cook in batches if needed.

2. For 1/4 lb. frozen burger patties: Air Fry at 360°F/180°C for a total of about 8-12 minutes. After the first 6 minutes flip the patties and continue to Air Frying at 360°F/180°C for another 2-6 minutes or until it's cooked to your preferred doneness. The internal temperature should be 160°F/71°C.

3. For 1/3 lb. frozen burger patties: Air Fry at 360°F/180°C for a total of about 12-16 minutes. After the first 10 minutes flip the patties and continue to Air Frying at 360°F/180°C for another 2-6 minutes or until it's cooked to your preferred doneness. The internal temperature should be 160°F/71°C.

4. For Cheeseburgers: add the slices of cheese on top of the cooked patties. Air fry at 360°F/180°C for about 30 seconds to 1 minute to melt the cheese.

5. Cover the patties and let rest for 3 minutes. Warm the buns in the air fryer at 380°F/193°C for about 3 minutes while patties are resting. Serve on buns, topped with your favorite burger toppings.

FISH & SEAFOOD RECIPES

Air Fryer Salmon In 6 Minutes Tender And Flaky

Servings: 4
Cooking Time: 6 Minutes

Ingredients:

- 4 fillets salmon 6 oz each
- 1 tablespoon olive oil
- 1/2 teaspoon salt
- 1/2 teaspoon pepper
- 2 tablespoons brown sugar
- 1/2 teaspoon smoked paprika
- 1/2 teaspoon garlic powder
- 1/2 teaspoon onion powder

Directions:

1. In a small bowl, coat the salmon with oil, then add the salt and pepper.
2. Mix the remaining sugar and spices and rub over the salmon.
3. Add the salmon skin side down to the air fryer basket and air fry at 200C/400F for 6 minutes, or until cooked.
4. Remove from the air fryer basket and sprinkle with chopped parsley.

Notes

TO STORE: Leftovers can be stored in an air-tight container in the refrigerator for up to 3 days.
TO FREEZE: Place the cooked and cooled salmon in a ziplock bag and store it in the freezer for up to two months.
TO REHEAT: Heat the leftovers gently in a skillet or pan on the stovetop over medium heat until hot.

Air Fryer Breaded Shrimp

Servings: 4
Cooking Time: 8 Minutes

Ingredients:

- 1 pound large raw shrimp peeled and deveined (I use 31/40 size)
- 1 cup Italian Breadcrumbs
- ¼ cup grated Parmesan cheese
- 1/2 cup all purpose flour
- 1/3 cup water
- 1/2 tsp dried parsley flakes
- 1/2 tsp paprika
- ½ tsp salt
- ¼ tsp ground black pepper
- 1 large egg

Directions:

1. In a shallow bowl, add breadcrumbs, parmesan cheese, parsley flakes, paprika, salt and pepper. Stir with a fork to combine ingredients.
2. In another large bowl, add the flour, egg, and water. Stir together to make a liquid batter.
3. Toss shrimp with the flour and egg batter, until they are coated on both sides.
4. Dredge each piece of shrimp in the panko mixture, coating both sides.
5. Lightly spray the air fryer basket, and place each shrimp into the basket, without stacking or overlapping.
6. Lightly spritz the coated shrimp with olive oil and then place shrimp in the air fryer basket. Air Fry at 380 degrees F for 8-10 minutes, flipping shrimp halfway through air frying.

Notes

Variations

Use panko breadcrumbs - Instead of using regular bread crumbs, you can use Panko bread crumbs.
Change the seasoning - Use Old Bay seasoning, lemon pepper, red pepper flakes, Cajun seasoning, and any

other flavors that you want to add to this shrimp recipe. The flavors take to the larger shrimp easily.

Make air fryer frozen shrimp - If you want to cook tender seafood, you can cook frozen shrimp in the air fryer as well. Just add them in a single layer in the basket of the air fryer.

Air Fryer Bacon Wrapped Shrimp

Servings: 4
Cooking Time: 10 Minutes

Ingredients:

- 24 shrimp
- 1 tbsp Old Bay seasoning
- 8 pieces bacon thinkly sliced, cut into thrids.

Directions:

1. Peel the shrimp and set them aside in a single layer onto a baking sheet.
2. Sprinkle a small amount of Old Bay Seasoning over the peeled shrimp.
3. Cut the bacon pieces into thirds. Carefully wrap the bacon around the shrimp, taking care to tuck the bacon under the bottom of the shrimp.
4. Prepare the basket of the air fryer with olive oil or with a nonstick cooking spray.
5. Add the bacon wrapped shrimp to the basket of the air fryer. Take care to keep the bacon edge tucked under the shrimp.
6. Cook on 390 degrees for 9-10 minutes, or until fully cooked.
7. Carefully remove the shrimp from the air fryer and serve immediately.

Notes

Bacon wrapped shrimp are delicious all by themselves, but they are also delicious when served with Remoulade sauce, sweet chili sauce, bbq sauce, dijon mustard, or teriyaki sauce.

Air Fryer Salmon

Servings: 4
Cooking Time: 10 Minutes

Ingredients:

- Salmon Seasoning
- 1 tablespoon paprika
- 1.5 tablespoons garlic powder
- 1 tablespoon brown sugar
- 2 teaspoons kosher salt
- 1 tablespoon dried thyme
- 1 teaspoon mustard powder
- 1 teaspoon black pepper
- Air Fryer Salmon
- 1.5 lbs. salmon filet sliced into 4 salmon steaks
- 1 tablespoon salmon seasoning
- 1 tablespoon olive oil

Directions:

1. First, combine all of the ingredients for the salmon seasoning. Mix to combine. Set aside. Note that you will have leftover salmon seasoning, so make sure to transfer the leftovers into a jar for later.
2. Preheat the air fryer to 400°F. Spray the air fryer basket with non-stick cooking spray.
3. Pat the salmon steaks with a paper towel to remove moisture and then sprinkle steaks with 1 tablespoon of salmon seasoning. Be sure each steak is coated in seasoning (don't worry about getting any of the seasoning on the skin).
4. Place the salmon skin-side down in the air fryer. Drizzle the salmon with the remaining olive oil. Be sure the salmon steaks are not overcrowded or touching (two batches may be needed depending on the size of the air fryer).
5. Cook the salmon for 7-8 minutes at 400°F.
6. Use a fork to test to see if the salmon is done. If that salmon flakes apart easily, remove it from the air fryer. If the salmon is not done, cook it for 1-minute increments until it is done cooking.
7. Let the salmon rest for 5 minutes and enjoy.

Tips & Notes

Want to cook from frozen? Place frozen salmon portions skin-side down onto your air fryer basket. Cook at 400°F for 7-9 minutes to defrost. Then, follow the recipe as directed.

The salmon seasoning becomes a delicious thin crust on the outside of the salmon. It creates a blackened look so don't be worried if it looks burnt.

Cajun Air Fryer Fish

Ingredients:

- Fresh fish fillets. Use any sustainable white fish. I used hake but halibut, cod, tilapia, bass, grouper, haddock, snapper or catfish will all work well.
- Olive oil - Vegetable oil like avocado oil is a good substitution
- Cajun seasoning/Cajun spice. Most supermarkets will have a cajun spice blend in their spice aisle.
- Smoked paprika
- Garlic powder. Onion powder can also be used
- Fresh lemon juice

Directions:

1. Slice the fish into portions then place in the air fryer basket. In a small bowl, mix the olive oil, lemon juice and seasonings together then spoon over the fish. I don't usually add parchment paper to the basket but you can if you're worried about the fish sticking. You can also spray the basket with cooking spray or olive oil. Air fry for 8-10 minutes at 200°C/400°F until the fish is caramelized on the outside and opaque and juicy on the inside. Cooking time will depend on the thickness of the fish but generally fish is cooked when it flakes apart easily and a fork can be inserted without any resistance. Remove from the air fryer then serve with lemon wedges.

Air Fryer Shrimp Fajitas

Servings: 4
Cooking Time: 8 Minutes

Ingredients:

- 1 lb shrimp fresh shrimp, peeled, tails off, deveined
- 1 medium red bell pepper
- 1 medium orange bell pepper
- 1 medium green bell pepper
- 1 medium yellow onion medium
- 2 tbsp fajita seasoning mix
- Toppings:
- 1 small avocado sliced
- 1 teaspoon cilantro fresh, chopped

Directions:

1. Cut the onion and bell peppers into strips and place them in a medium bowl.
2. Rinse the shrimp under water in a colander and then place on a paper towel to pat dry. Add to the bowl with the shrimp.
3. Add the fajita seasoning to the shrimp and bell peppers and toss to coat them evenly.
4. Add the shrimp, peppers, and onion to the basket of the air fryer.
5. Air fry the shrimp and vegetables at 400 degrees Fahrenheit for 8 minutes, tossing the mixture halfway through the cooking process.
6. Carefully remove from the air fryer and serve on a flour tortilla and top with your favorite toppings.

Notes

This easy air fryer shrimp recipe can be served any way that you want. You can add the ingredients to a large bowl and top it with sour cream, cayenne pepper, and more. It's simple to turn this dish into air fryer shrimp fajita bowls.

You can also get flour tortillas or corn tortillas and fill them fully! Perfect for busy weeknights.

The best way to serve this recipe is to let everyone add their own toppings and enjoy.

Air Fryer Frozen Shrimp

Cooking Time: 8 Minutes

Ingredients:

- 16 ounces breaded frozen shrimp
- non-stick cooking spray
- squeeze of lemon, optional

Directions:

1. Preheat the air fryer to 400 degrees Fahrenheit.
2. Add the frozen shrimp to the air fryer tray or basket in a single layer. Spray with non-stick cooking spray if you want it crispy.
3. Close the basket and cook in the air fryer for 8 minutes flipping the shrimp halfway through at the 4-minute mark.
4. Serve with a squeeze of lemon and dipping sauce on the side!

Frozen Shrimp In The Air Fryer

Servings: 4

Cooking Time: 7 Minutes

Ingredients:

- 1 pound frozen cooked large shrimp
- 1 tablespoon unsalted butter, melted
- 1 tablespoon Old Bay seasoning
- ½ tablespoon lemon juice
- 1 teaspoon minced garlic

Directions:

1. Heat air fryer to 350 degrees F.
2. Break apart frozen shrimp and place the shrimp, butter, Old Bay seasoning, lemon juice, and garlic in a large bowl. Stir to combine and coat all of the shrimp.
3. In a single layer lay your shrimp (about ½ a pound per batch) and cook for 6 to 7 minutes until fully heated.

Air-fried Beer Battered Fish Tacos With Mango Salsa Recipe

Ingredients:

- For the fish:
- 2 eggs
- 10 ounces of Mexican beer
- 1 1/2 cups of corn starch
- 1 1/2 cups of flour
- 1/2 tablespoon of chili powder
- 1 tablespoon of cumin
- Kosher salt and fresh cracked pepper to taste
- 1 pound of cod cut into large pieces
- Non-stick spray
- For the Salsa & to make the Taco:
- 3 peeled and medium-diced mangos
- 1/2 peeled, seeded and small diced red bell pepper
- 1 peeled, seeded and small diced jalapeno
- 1/2 peeled and small diced red onion
- 1 tablespoon of chopped fresh cilantro
- Juice of 1 lime
- Kosher salt and fresh cracked pepper to taste
- 1/2 thinly sliced head of red cabbage
- Soft corn tortillas
- Crumbled queso fresco for garnish
- Sliced green onions and cilantro leaves for garnish

Directions:

1. For the salsa:
2. Combine the mangos, peppers, onion, chopped cilantro, lime juice together in a medium size bowl and mix. Refrigerate until ready to serve.
3. For the fish:
4. In a medium size bowl whisk together the eggs and beer and set aside.
5. In a separate medium bowl whisk together the cornstarch, flour, chili powder, cumin, salt and pepper.
6. Coat the fish in the egg-beer mixture and transfer it to the flour mixture and dredge to completely coat on all sides.

7. Spray the bottom of the air fryer basket with no-stick spray and place in the fish and spray the tops of the fish with no-stick spray.

8. Cook at 375 degrees for 15 minutes

9. Place the air fried fish on a corn tortilla and top off with cabbage, salsa, queso fresco, green onions, and cilantro.

10. Enjoy!

Air Fryer Cod

Servings: 4

Cooking Time: 10 Minutes

Ingredients:

- 4 125g Fresh Cod loins: you can substitute for fillets too
- 30 g melted unsalted butter
- 1 Lemon sliced
- Salt to taste
- black pepper to taste

Directions:

1. Preheat the air fryer at 200C/400F for 5 minutes.

2. Pat the cod fillets dry so it is moist-free. Season the fish generously with salt and black pepper then brush the melted butter on one side of the fish

3. Spray the air fryer basket with cooking oil. Place the cod fillet/loin in the air fryer basket buttered side down making sure they are not touching. Brush the remaining butter on top of the fish, add one lemon slice each to the fish

4. Cook for 10 minutes, carefully remove the fish and transfer to a plate. Serve with lemon butter sauce, roasted potatoes and veggies and enjoy!

Notes

Check on the cod earlier than the time specified for this recipe so as not to overcook the fish. Remember, the thickness of your fish would determine how long it cooks in an air fryer. see the timing on this recipe as a guide. A good starting point to start checking on the fish is from 6 minutes.

As with the majority of air fryer recipes, do not overcrowd the air fryer basket so as to allow the food to cook evenly.

Customise the seasoning to taste.

Let the cod come to room temperature a few minutes before you cook for accurate cooking. The temperature of cooked fish should register at 145F/62C.

Do not leave the fish in the air fryer once the cooking is completed otherwise the fish would overcook and maybe even dry out.

Don't own an air fryer but would like to try this recipe, bake in the oven @200C/400F for 10 minutes. You can also cook your fresh or frozen cod in an air fryer in under 3 minutes.

Air Fryer Crispy Fish Fillets

Servings: 3

Cooking Time: 15 Minutes

Ingredients:

- 1 pound (454 g) white fish fillets (cod, halibut, tilapia, etc.)
- 1 teaspoon (5 ml) kosher salt , or to taste
- 1/2 teaspoon (2.5 ml) black pepper , or to taste
- 1 teaspoon (5 ml) garlic powder
- 1 teaspoon (5 ml) paprika
- 1-2 cups (60-120 g) breading of choice breadcrumbs, panko, crushed pork rinds or almond flour
- 1 egg , or more if needed
- Cooking Spray
- EQUIPMENT
- Air Fryer
- Air Fryer Parchment Paper (optional)
- Perforated Silicone Mats (optional)

Directions:

1. Preheat the Air Fryer at 380°F/193°C for 4 minutes.

2. If using frozen filets, make sure to thaw first. Cut fish filets in half if needed. Make sure they are even sized so they'll cook evenly. The thicker they are, the longer they will take to cook. Pat the filets dry. Lightly oil the filets and then season with the salt, black pepper, garlic powder, and paprika.

3. Put the breading in a shallow bowl. In another bowl, beat the eggs. Dip the filets in the egg, shaking off

excess egg. Dredge the filets in your breading of choice. Press filets into the bowl of breading so that they completely coat the filets. Repeat this process for all fish pieces.

4. Line air fryer basket or tray with perforated parchment paper or perforated silicone mat (highly recommended - if you don't have perforated parchment paper or mat, make sure to generously coat the air fryer basket with oil spray). Lightly spray parchment paper with oil spray. Lay coated fish in a single layer on the parchment (cook in batches if needed). Generously spray all sides of the breaded filets with oil spray to coat any dry spots.

5. Air Fry at 380°F/193°C for 8-14 minutes, depending on the size and thickness of your filets. After 6 minutes, flip the filets. Lightly spray any dry spots than then continue cooking for the remaining time or until they are crispy brown and the fish is cooked through. Serve with your favorite dip: tartar sauce, mustard, aioli, etc.

Air Fried Coconut Shrimp

Ingredients:
- 1 pound deveined and peeled jumbo shrimp
- 1/3 cup flour
- 1/2 tsp salt
- 1/2 tsp pepper
- 2 large eggs, beaten,
- 3/4 cup panko breadcrumbs
- 1 cup sweetened shredded coconut
- Vegetable oil or coconut oil

Directions:
1. Rinse shrimp under cold water and pat dry with a towel.
2. Combine flour, salt and pepper in a me dium bowl. Beat eggs in a second bowl.
3. Combine panko and coconut in a third bowl.
4. Dip the shrimp into the flour, then the eggs, and then into the coconut mixture, pressing gently.
5. Lightly oil the mesh basket to prevent sticking and add the battered shrimp.

6. Air fry at 350°F for 4 minutes. Turn shrimp and continue to cook for 3 minutes or until crispy.

Air Fryer Honey Mustard Salmon Recipe

Servings: 3
Cooking Time: 10 Minutes

Ingredients:
- 3 salmon fillets 1 ½ inches thick
- salt and pepper
- 2 tablespoons honey
- 1 tablespoon Dijon mustard

Directions:
1. Make a foil sling for the air fryer basket, about 4 inches tall and a few inches longer than the width of the basket. Lay foil widthwise across basket, pressing it into and up the sides. Lightly spray foil and basket with cooking spray.
2. Pat salmon dry with paper towels. Season with salt and pepper.
3. In a small bowl, mix together honey and Dijon, until well combined. Reserve 1 tablespoon of glaze. Drizzle remaining glaze evenly over salmon fillets, tops and sides.
4. Arrange fillets skin side down on sling in the basket, with space between them. (The number of fillets you can fit in your air fryer at one time depends on the size of the fillets and the size of your air fryer.)
5. Cook at 350°F/175°C for 8-10 minutes, until salmon flakes easily and registers at 145˚F/62.8˚C (thinner salmon will be ready sooner, thicker salmon will take more time).
6. Using sling, carefully lift salmon from air fryer. Loosen the skin with a fish spatula or utensil, then transfer fillets to plate, leaving skin behind.
7. Drizzle reserved sauce over fillets. Garnish with fresh parsley, if desired. Serve warm.

Air Fryer Fish & Chips

Servings: 2

Cooking Time: 25 Minutes

Ingredients:

- Chips:
- 2 large potatoes, scrubbed, dried & sliced into chunky chips
- 1 Tbsp olive oil
- Salt, to taste
- Fish:
- 2 x 200g kingklip fillets (or similar firm white fish)
- 1 cup flour
- 1 XL egg, whisked
- ½ cup panko breadcrumbs
- ½ tsp sweet paprika
- ½ tsp garlic powder
- Salt and pepper, to taste
- Tartar sauce:
- 200ml mayonnaise
- 3 Tbsp baby capers, roughly chopped
- 3 Tbsp gherkins, finely minced
- 2 Tbsp fresh parsley, finely minced
- 1 Tbsp lemon zest
- 1 Tbsp lemon juice
- Lemon wedges, to serve

Directions:

1. In a bowl combine the potatoes, olive oil and salt.
2. Toss well to coat.
3. Spread out on one of the slotted Vortex Oven baking trays.
4. Set the Vortex Oven to Air Fry for 10 min at 202°C.
5. Once preheated add the chips in the bottom half of the oven, above the solid baking tray.
6. Place flour and whisked egg in 2 shallow bowls.
7. In a third shallow bowl combine the panko breadcrumbs, paprika, garlic powder and a little salt and pepper. Mix.
8. Season the fish fillets with salt and pepper.
9. Dip each piece in flour, shake off any excess, followed by egg and then the seasoned breadcrumbs.
10. Place the fish pieces onto a slotted Vortex Oven baking tray, allowing room in between each piece for proper air circulation.
11. Once the chips have finished their initial 10 minutes, immediately add the fish to the upper half of the oven. Set the Vortex Oven to Air Fry for another 10 min at 202°C. Turn halfway through.
12. While the fish is cooking combine the mayonnaise, capers, gherkins, parsley, lemon zest and lemon juice in a bowl. Mix well.
13. Serve fish and chips fresh out of the oven with a dollop of tartar sauce and a generous squeeze of lemon.

Air Fryer Keto Coconut Shrimp

Servings: 8

Cooking Time: 10 Minutes

Ingredients:

- 25 large shrimp peeled and deveined
- 1/2 cup coconut flour
- 1 3/4 cup coconut flakes unsweetened
- 3 eggs
- 1 tbsp ground black pepper
- 1 tsp smoked paprika
- 1 tsp salt

Directions:

1. Preheat the Air Fryer to 390 degrees Fahrenheit. Prepare the air fryer basket with non stick cooking spray.
2. Arrange three bowls. Add the coconut flour, paprika, salt and pepper to one bowl. Coconut flakes to the second bowl, and beaten eggs in the third bowl.
3. Dip the shrimp into the coconut flour mixture, then dip into the egg mixture, and finally into the coconut flakes. Set aside on a wire rack until you've finished with all of the shrimp.
4. Add the coconut shrimp in a single layer into the prepared air fryer basket and cook for 8-10 minutes at 380 degrees Fahrenheit. Flip the shrimp halfway through.
5. Remove when golden brown and serve immediately.

Notes

If you have any "hanging" coconut flakes they will likely brown faster than the shrimp. Air fryers also cook differently and have different wattages. You may need to add or take away time for this recipe depending on the type of air fryer you own.

Air Fryer Shrimp Skewers

Servings: 4

Cooking Time: 9 Minutes

Ingredients:

- 20 large shrimp fresh, peeled

Directions:

1. Soak the wooden skewers in water for 20 minutes.
2. Rinse the shrimp and pat them dry with a paper towel.
3. Place the shrimp on the wooden skewers and then add them in a single layer in the air fryer basket.
4. Air fry the shrimp at 380 degrees Fahrenheit for 8-9 minutes.
5. Carefully remove the shrimp from the air fryer and serve.

Notes

Serve shrimp skewers over rice, roasted vegetables, or by themselves with cocktail sauce. You can also serve these air fried shrimp over a salad or for shrimp tacos.

You can season the shrimp however you desire. Add a little lemon pepper seasoning, or Old Bay seasoning before cooking. You can also just opt for a little salt and pepper. It's up to you and how you would like to serve them.

Air Fryer Shrimp

Servings: 4

Cooking Time: 7 Minutes

Ingredients:

- 1 lb shrimp large or extra large
- 1 tablespoon olive oil
- 1/2 tablespoon lemon juice
- 1/2 teaspoon salt
- 1/2 teaspoon pepper
- 1/2 teaspoon garlic

- 1/2 teaspoon smoked paprika
- 1 teaspoon Italian seasonings

Directions:

1. Pat dry shrimp with a paper towel.
2. In a mixing bowl, whisk together the olive oil and lemon juice. Add the seasonings and mix well. Toss through the shrimp in the seasoning mix.
3. Cook the shrimp at 200C/400F for 7-8 minutes.
4. Serve immediately.

Notes

TO STORE: Air fryer shrimp can be stored in the refrigerator for up to 3 days in an air-tight container.

TO FREEZE: Place leftovers in a ziplock bag and store it in the freezer for up to 2 months.

TO REHEAT: Thaw and then put on the baking sheet or in the air fryer basket to reheat until crispy.

Air Fryer Coconut Shrimp

Servings: 4

Ingredients:

- FOR THE SHRIMP
- 1/2 c. all-purpose flour
- Kosher salt
- Freshly ground black pepper
- 1 c. panko bread crumbs
- 1/2 c. shredded sweetened coconut
- 2 large eggs, beaten
- 1 lb. large tail-on shrimp, peeled and deveined
- 1/2 c. mayonnaise
- 1 tbsp. sriracha
- 1 tbsp. Thai sweet chili sauce

Directions:

1. In a shallow bowl, season flour with salt and black pepper. In another shallow bowl, combine panko and coconut. In a third shallow bowl, beat eggs to blend.
2. Working one at a time, dip shrimp into seasoned flour, shaking off any excess. Dip into eggs, then into panko mixture, gently pressing to adhere.
3. Working in batches if necessary, in an air-fryer basket, arrange shrimp in a single layer. Cook at

400° until shrimp is golden brown and cooked through, 7 to 9 minutes.

4. In a small bowl, combine mayonnaise, sriracha, and chili sauce.

5. Arrange shrimp on a platter. Serve with dipping sauce alongside.

Crisp-skinned Air Fryer Salmon With Salsa Verde

Servings: 4
Cooking Time: 25 Minutes

Ingredients:

- 4 x 185g salmon fillets, skin on
- 1 tablespoon extra virgin olive oil
- 2 teaspoon sea salt flakes
- 1 small shallot, chopped finely
- 1 clove garlic, crushed
- 2 teaspoon finely grated lemon rind
- 2 tablespoon lemon juice
- 2 tablespoon finely chopped dill
- ¼ cup chopped flat-leaf parsley
- 2 tablespoon chopped chives
- 1 tablespoon baby capers, chopped coarsely
- to serve: extra sea salt flakes

Directions:

1. Preheat a 7-litre air fryer to 200°C/400°F for 3 minutes.

2. Rub salmon with oil, then sprinkle with salt flakes.

3. Taking care, line the air fryer basket with a silicone mat, if available. Place salmon, skin-side up, in the basket; at 200°C/400°F, cook for 8 minutes until skin is crisp and salmon is cooked to your liking.

4. Meanwhile, to make salsa verde, combine remaining ingredients in a medium bowl; mix well. Season.

5. Serve salmon topped with salsa verde and sprinkled with extra salt flakes.

Air Fryer Salmon And Swiss Chard

Servings: 4

Ingredients:

- 1 medium red onion (sliced 1/2 inch thick)
- 1 1/2 tbsp. oil, divided
- Kosher salt and pepper
- 1 large bunch red Swiss chard (thick stems discarded, leaves chopped)
- 2 cloves garlic (sliced)
- 4 5-oz. salmon fillets
- Chili oil, for serving

Directions:

1. Heat air fryer to 385°F. Toss onion with 1/2 tablespoon oil and a pinch each of salt and pepper and air-fry 5 minutes.

2. Toss with Swiss chard, garlic, 1 tablespoon oil, and 1/4 teaspoon each salt and pepper and air-fry until chard and onion are just tender, about 5 minutes more. Transfer to plates.

3. Season salmon with 1/2 teaspoon each salt and pepper and air-fry at 400°F until skin is crispy and salmon is opaque throughout, 8 to 10 minutes. Serve with chard and drizzle with chili oil if desired.

Air Fryer Bacon Wrapped Scallops

Servings: 4
Cooking Time: 13 Minutes

Ingredients:

- 16 large sea scallops cleaned & pat dry with paper towels
- 8 slices center cut bacon
- 1/4 cup Williamson Bros. BBQ sauce

Directions:

1. Slice bacon in half and place the bacon in the air fryer to partially cook at 400 for 3 minutes.

2. 16 large sea scallops

3. Pat the scallops dry with paper towels to remove any moisture.

4. Wrap each scallop in 1/2 slice of bacon and secure it with a toothpick.

5. 8 slices center cut bacon

6. Place scallops in air fryer (I can fit 8 at a time in my basket style air fryer)

7. Lightly brush scallop with your favorite barbecue sauce. I recommend a thinner sauce – not a heavy thick sauce. You can also just spray with olive oil and salt/pepper.

8. Cook at 400 for 5 minutes. Turn scallops delicately and baste again with bbq sauce. Cook for another 5 minutes at 400 until scallop is tender and opaque and bacon is cooked through. Serve hot.

9. 1/4 cup Williamson Bros. BBQ sauce

10. I also sprinkled a little Historic BBQ Red seasoning on them when they were done.

Air Fryer Lobster Tail

Servings: 4

Cooking Time: 5 Minutes

Ingredients:

- 4 5-oz Lobster tails
- 1/4 cup Salted butter (melted; 1/2 stick)
- 2 cloves Garlic (crushed)
- 2 tsp Lemon juice
- 1/2 tsp Smoked paprika
- 1 pinch Cayenne pepper (or more if you want extra heat)

Directions:

1. If tails are frozen, thaw them overnight in the fridge, or in a bag submerged in cold water on the counter for about 30 minutes.

2. Preheat the air fryer to 400 degrees F (204 degrees C)for a few minutes.

3. Butterfly the lobster tails. Using kitchen shears, cut down the center of the shell lengthwise, starting from the end opposite the tail fins, continuing down until you reach the tail but without cutting the tail. You want to cut through the top of the shell, but don't cut through the bottom shell. Use your thumbs and fingers to spread open the shell on top, then use your thumbs and fingers to spread open the shell. Run a bamboo skewer through the center of the flesh lengthwise to prevent curling.

4. In a small bowl, whisk together the melted butter, garlic, lemon juice, smoked paprika, and cayenne. Brush the butter mixture over the lobster meat.

5. Cook lobster tails in the air fryer for 5-6 minutes for 5-ounce lobster tails, or until the meat is opaque and internal temperature in the thickest part reaches 140 degrees F (60 degrees C). (If your tails are a different size, a good rule of thumb for lobster tail air fryer time is about 1 minute per ounce of individual tail. For example, if your lobster tails are 8 ounces each, you'll air fry them for about 8 minutes.) After cooking for 1 minute per ounce of individual tail, check the internal temperature with a meat thermometer and if they are not done yet, cook for 1-3 more minutes as needed.

Fish 'n' Chips

Servings: 4

Ingredients:

- For the chips
- 700g King Edward or Maris Piper potatoes
- 2 tbsp sunflower oil
- Sea salt
- 2 tsp semolina (optional)
- lemon wedges and parsley to garnish
- For the fish
- 2 slices stale bread, crusts removed and torn into pieces
- 1 garlic clove
- 1 zest of lemon
- 5g fresh parsley, leaves and stalks
- sea salt and pepper to taste
- 1 x 120g chunky thick skinless cod fillets, pat dry
- 2 tbsp oil
- COOKING MODE
- When entering cooking mode - We will enable your screen to stay 'always on' to avoid any unnecessary interruptions whilst you cook!

Directions:

1. Peel potatoes and cut into 5cm thick chips. Place in a bowl, cover with water and allow to soak for 30

minutes to remove excess starch. Rinse and pat potatoes dry.

2. In a clean bowl, add chips, oil, salt and semolina. Toss together to make sure the chips are coated. Insert crisper plates into both drawers and add the chips to Zone 1 drawer.

3. Place bread, garlic, lemon, parsley and seasoning into a food processor. Whizz until you have fine breadcrumbs. Add oil and pulse until mixed. Spoon breadcrumb topping onto cod. Press topping on with the back of spoon. Spray Zone 2 drawer and carefully place topped cod into drawer.

4. Select Zone 1, turn the dial to select AIR FRY, set temperature to 200°C, and set time to 26 minutes. Select Zone 2 and turn the dial to select ROAST, set temperature to 170°C and set time to 14 minutes. Select SYNC. Press the dial to begin cooking.

5. After 10 minutes, shake Zone 1 drawer, shake again after 15 and 20 minutes. Check at 24 minutes if cooked enough.

6. When cooking time is complete, remove fish and chips and serve with tartar sauce and mushy peas.

POULTRY RECIPES

Bbq Chicken In Air Fryer

Servings: 4
Cooking Time: 20 Minutes

Ingredients:

- 4-6 pieces chicken drumsticks
- 2 tablespoons brown sugar
- 1 teaspoon garlic powder
- 1 tablespoon olive oil or non-stick spray
- 1/2 cup BBQ Sauce

Directions:

1. To prepare the basket or air fryer trays, brush about ½ tablespoon olive oil or spray with cooking spray.
2. Place the chicken, in a single layer, in the air fryer basket. Avoid stacking or overlapping any pieces of chicken.
3. To prepare the chicken dry rub, use a small bowl and blend together the brown sugar and teaspoon garlic powder. Sprinkle the spice mix over each piece of chicken on both sides. Pat it down until the chicken is well covered.
4. Air fry the chicken at 400 degrees Fahrenheit for 20 minutes cooking time. Flip the chicken over halfway through cooking. Use a meat thermometer to confirm internal temperature of 165 degrees F.
5. Once done cooking, remove chicken pieces from air fryer basket or air fryer trays, and then brush chicken with barbecue sauce on both sides of each piece.
6. Serve immediately.

Notes

I use a Cosori air fryer to make these BBQ Chicken Drumsticks. 20 minutes was perfect timing 4-6 pieces of chicken. Cook times may vary depending on size, wattage, and thickness of your chicken. You may need to give chicken extra 1-2 minutes of cooking time. The safest way to confirm doneness when cooking meat is to use a digital meat thermometer like this one. The thickest part of the chicken should have internal temperature of 165 degrees Fahrenheit.

For extra flavor, you can add cayenne pepper or chili powder.

Air Fryer Popcorn Chicken With Jalapeño Ranch

Servings: 6
Cooking Time: 15 Minutes

Ingredients:

- 500 g (1lb) chicken breasts
- 1 cup flour
- 2 eggs beaten
- 2 cups panko breadcrumbs
- 1 tsp salt
- 1 tsp smoked paprika
- 1 tsp garlic powder
- 1 tsp dried oregano
- 1 tsp pepper
- For the Jalapeño Ranch
- ½ cup sour cream
- ½ cup mayonnaise
- 1 tbsp Jalapeños chopped
- 2 tsp dill finely chopped
- 1 tsp parsley finely chopped
- 2 tsp chives finely chopped
- 1-2 tsp lime juice
- salt and pepper to taste

Directions:

1. Slice the chicken into bite size chunks.
2. Place the flour, eggs and panko breadcrumbs in separate shallow bowls. Season the flour with salt and pepper. Season the breadcrumbs with the spices.
3. Coat the chicken in the flour, then in the beaten egg and finally in the breadcrumbs mixture. For a thicker coating, repeat the egg and breadcrumb steps.

4. Place the chicken pieces in a single layer in the basket of an air fryer then drizzle or spray with olive oil.
5. Cook the chicken at 200°C/390°F for 15 minutes, turning half way through.
6. Finely chop the herbs and place in a bowl. Mix in the mayonnaise, sour cream, lime juice, jalapeños, salt and pepper. Taste and adjust seasoning if necessary.
7. Remove the popcorn chicken from the air fryer then serve with the ranch and lime wedges.

Broccoli And Cheese Stuffed Chicken

Servings: 4
Cooking Time: 25 Minutes

Ingredients:

- 2 cups finely chopped broccoli floret
- 8 thin chicken breast cutlets (about 3 to 4 ounces each)
- 1 large egg
- 2 teaspoons water
- 3/4 cup whole wheat or gluten-free seasoned breadcrumbs
- 4 slices cheddar cheese (cut in half 3 oz)
- 3/4 teaspoon kosher salt
- olive oil spray
- toothpicks

Directions:

1. OVEN Directions:
2. Preheat oven to 425F. Spray a sheet pan with oil.
3. Place broccoli in the microwave with 1 tablespoon water, cover and cook 1 minute until soft. Drain and season with 1/4 teaspoon salt.
4. In a small bowl, combine egg, water and a little salt and beat with a fork; set aside. Fill a second bowl with breadcrumbs.
5. If the chicken isn't 1/4-inch thin, pound it thin with wax paper and a mallet. Season both sides of the chicken with 1/2 teaspoon salt. Place a 1/2 slice cheese in the center of the chicken and top with 2 tablespoons broccoli.
6. Roll the chicken around to completely cover cheese, using toothpicks to secure the ends, if needed.
7. Dip chicken into egg wash, then breadcrumbs and transfer to a sheet pan. Spray both sides of the chicken with oil and bake about 25 minutes, until cooked. Remove toothpicks and eat.
8. AIR FRYER RECIPE:
9. Preheat air fryer to 400F. Spray a sheet pan with oil.
10. Place broccoli in the microwave with 1 tablespoon water, cover and cook 1 minute until soft. Drain and season with 1/4 teaspoon salt.
11. In a small bowl, combine egg, water and a little salt and beat with a fork; set aside. Fill a second bowl with breadcrumbs.
12. If the chicken isn't thin enough to easily roll, pound it thin with wax paper and a mallet. Season both sides of the chicken with 1/2 teaspoon salt. Place a 1/2 slice cheese in the center of the chicken and top with 2 tablespoons broccoli.
13. Roll the chicken around to completely cover cheese, using toothpicks to secure the ends, if needed.
14. Dip chicken into egg wash, then breadcrumbs and transfer to a work surface. Spray both sides of the chicken with oil and transfer to the air fryer basket, in batches. Cook about 14 to 16 minutes, turning halfway until the chicken is cooked through in the center. Remove toothpicks before eating.

Butter Chicken

Servings: 6
Cooking Time: 30 Minutes

Ingredients:

- 1 ½ pounds boneless, skinless chicken breast, cut into 1-inch pieces
- Kosher salt, as needed
- 3 tablespoons ghee
- ½ cup shallots, thinly sliced
- 1 can fire roasted crushed tomatoes (28 ounces)
- 1 ½ tablespoons fresh ginger, grated
- 6 garlic cloves, minced

- 1 tablespoons ground fenugreek
- 2 ½ teaspoons kosher salt, plus more as needed
- 2 teaspoon ground paprika
- 2 teaspoons turmeric
- 1 teaspoon ground cumin
- ½ teaspoon ground cardamom
- ¼ teaspoon ground cloves
- 1/3 cup cashew butter
- 1 cup chicken stock
- 1 can coconut milk (15 ounces)
- 2 tablespoons fresh cilantro, chopped, for serving
- Warm naan bread, for serving
- Items Needed:
- Blender

Directions:

1. Season the chicken generously with kosher salt.
2. Select the Sauté Function on the Pressure Cooker and press Temp Set, then customize the temperature to high and time to 12 minutes.
3. Add 2 tablespoons of ghee into the pressure cooker, then sear off the chicken in batches, removing the chicken to a plate as each piece is golden brown on all sides.
4. Add the remaining ghee and the shallots into the inner pot and cook, stirring occasionally, until the shallots are translucent, then stir in the garlic, ginger, and spices, followed by the cashew butter. Pour in the tomatoes and chicken stock stir to dissolve the cashew butter, then add the chicken pieces back into the pot.
5. Place the lid onto the pressure cooker.
6. Select the Pressure function, adjust pressure to high, and time to 15 minutes, then press Start.
7. Slowly release pressure by sliding the vent switch in between Seal and Vent. Slide the switch to Vent after 15 minutes.
8. Open the lid carefully.
9. Stir the coconut milk into the sauce, then adjust the seasoning to taste with kosher salt.
10. Serve the butter chicken on plates with naan, garnished with cilantro.

Air Fryer Chicken, Broccoli, And Onions

Servings: 4

Cooking Time: 20 Minutes

Ingredients:

- 1 pound (454 g) boneless skinless chicken breast or thighs , cut into 1-inch bites sized pieces
- 1/4-1/2 pound (113-227 g) broccoli , cut into florets (1-2 cups)
- 1/2 onion , sliced thick
- 3 Tablespoons (45 ml) vegetable oil or grape seed oil
- 1/2 teaspoon (2.5 ml) garlic powder
- 1 Tablespoon (15 ml) fresh minced ginger
- 1 Tablespoon (15 ml) soy sauce , or to taste (use Tamari for Gluten Free)
- 1 Tablespoon (15 ml) rice vinegar (use distilled white vinegar for Gluten Free)
- 1 teaspoon (5 ml) sesame oil
- 2 teaspoons (10 ml) hot sauce (optional)
- 1/2 teaspoon (2.5 ml) sea salt , or to taste
- black pepper , to taste
- serve with lemon wedges , optional

Directions:

1. AIR FRYING OPTION #1: REGULAR COOKED BROCCOLI
2. Make Marinade: In a bowl, combine oil, garlic powder, ginger, soy sauce, rice vinegar, sesame oil, optional hot sauce, salt, and pepper.
3. In bowl add chicken. In a second bowl add broccoli and onions. Divide the marinade between the two bowls, stirring to coat each completely.
4. Air Fry: Add just the chicken to the air fryer basket/tray. Air Fry at 380°F/195°C for 10 minutes. Stir in the broccoli and onions with the chicken (make sure to include all the marinade). Continue to Air Fry at 380°F/195°C for 8-10 minutes, or until the chicken is cooked through. Make sure to stir halfway through cooking so broccoli gets cooked evenly.

5. Season with additional salt and pepper, to taste. Add fresh lemon juice on top (optional) and serve warm.

6. AIR FRYING OPTION #2: EXTRA CRISPY, CHARRED BROCCOLI

7. Combine chicken, broccoli and onion in bowl. Toss ingredients together.

8. Make Marinade: In a bowl, combine oil, garlic powder, ginger, soy sauce, rice vinegar, sesame oil, optional hot sauce, salt, and pepper. Add the chicken, broccoli and onions to the marinade. Stir thoroughly to combine the marinade with chicken, broccoli and onions.

9. Air Fry: Add ingredients to air fryer basket/tray. Air Fry 380°F/195°C for 16-20 minutes, shaking and gently tossing halfway through cooking. Make sure to toss so that everything cooks evenly. Check chicken to make sure it's cooked through. If not, cook for additional 3-5 minutes.

10. If needed, season with additional salt and pepper, to taste. Add fresh lemon juice on top (optional) and serve warm.

Notes

Air Frying Tips and Notes:Shake or turn as directed in the recipe. Don't overcrowd the air fryer basket.Recipes were tested in 3.4 to 6 qt air fryers. If using a larger air fryer, the recipe might cook quicker so adjust cooking time.Remember to set a timer to shake/flip/toss as directed in recipe.

Air Fryer Chili Crisp Crunch Chicken Wings

Servings: 4

Cooking Time: 30 Minutes

Ingredients:

- 2 pounds (907 g) chicken wings
- Kosher salt , or sea salt, to taste
- black pepper , to taste
- garlic powder , optional
- 1/4 cup chili crisp crunch , or to taste
- OPTIONAL - FOR EXTRA CRISPY CORN STARCH CRUST

- 1/4 cup (30 g) corn starch , or as needed
- oil spray , as needed
- EQUIPMENT
- Air Fryer
- Oil Sprayer optional

Directions:

1. If you have whole wings, separate them into the drum and flat. If needed, pat dry the chicken wings. Season with salt, pepper, and optional garlic powder.

2. For oil-free version, place in even layer in air fryer basket/tray. Follow air fry instructions below. For Extra Crispy Crust, follow optional steps for corn starch crust.

3. FOR EXTRA CRISPY CORN STARCH CRUST

4. Add seasoning to the wings then lay them in single layer on a plate or cutting board. Sprinkle cornstarch over the wings on both sides.

5. Liberally spray wings evenly with oil spray so that all the cornstarch is coated in oil. There should be no dry white clumps of cornstarch or else they will cook hard and dry.

6. Place the coated wings in your air fryer basket or tray/rack.

7. AIR FRY

8. Air Fry wings at 400°F/205°C for 20 minutes minutes or until crispy-looking and nearly cooked through.

9. Flip the wings and Air Fry at 400°F/205°C for additional 5-10 minutes or until wings are fully cooked and crispy.

10. Toss with the chili crisp/crunch to taste. Spiciness will vary greatly on the brand of chili crisp/crunch, as well has how much you use on the wings. Adjust to your preference.

Notes

No Oil Necessary. The wings have enough fat in the skin to crisp up nicely on their own.

Shake several times for even cooking.

Don't overcrowd fryer basket.

If using a sauce, it is added in just at the end, otherwise it often burns before the chicken wings are cooked.

Recipes were cooked in 3-4 qt air fryers. If using a larger air fryer, the recipe might cook quicker so adjust cooking time.

If cooking in multiple batches, the first batch will take longer to cook if Air Fryer is not already pre-heated.

Remember to set a timer to shake/flip/toss the food as directed in recipe.

Air Fryer Chicken Parmesan

Servings: 4

Cooking Time: 35 Minutes

Ingredients:

- 2 boneless, skinless chicken breasts
- 1 cup bread crumbs (regular, panko, or combo)
- ½ cup shredded Parmesan cheese, divided
- 2 teaspoons Italian seasoning
- 1 teaspoon garlic powder
- ½ teaspoon kosher salt
- 2 large eggs
- ½ cup marinara sauce, plus more for serving
- ½ mozzarella cheese, shredded

Directions:

1. Preheat your air fryer to 350 degrees. Cut the chicken breasts in half horizontally, pounding them to even thickness as needed; set aside.
2. In a shallow bowl, combine bread crumbs, all but 2 tablespoons of Parmesan, Italian seasoning, garlic powder, and salt. In a second bowl, whisk the eggs.
3. Dip each piece of chicken in the egg, and let the excess egg drip off. Press the chicken pieces into the breadcrumb mixture, coating evenly.
4. Place the chicken in a single layer in the air fryer. Spray the top of the chicken with cooking spray. (You will likely need to do this in batches.)
5. Air fry for 8-11 minutes, flipping halfway, until the chicken is golden and mostly cooked through. Carefully spread 2 tablespoons of marinara sauce over each breast, then sprinkle with mozzarella. Continue cooking for 2-3 minutes, until the cheese is melted and the chicken is cooked through to 165 degrees F.

Crispy Sesame Chicken

Ingredients:

- 1kg chicken pieces of your choice
- (I used drumsticks and chicken fillet)
- Salt and Pepper for seasoning
- 3 tablespoons cornflour
- 3 eggs
- 3 cups flour
- 3 tablespoons barbecue spice
- 3 teaspoon paprika
- 3 tablespoons sesame seeds
- 1 tablespoon mixed herbs
- Olive oil spray

Directions:

1. Cut the chicken fillets into strips and make 2 slits across the top of the drumsticks. In a medium bowl whisk together the egg with a dash of milk.
2. In a separate large bowl add together the flour spices, herbs and sesame seeds. Mix until well combined. Line a tray with baking paper or cling wrap. Rinse the chicken and pat dry with roller towel, season with salt and pepper and dust with the cornflour. Dip the chicken in the beaten egg and then in the flour mixture and transfer to the lined tray. Once all the chicken is evenly coated, transfer to the tray. Pop the chicken in the freezer for 20 minutes and allow the coating to set. (If you resting chicken for longer than 20 minutes pop the chicken in the fridge and not freezer)
3. After 20 minutes spray both sides of the chicken with olive oil and air fry in the Vortex Air fryer on 200 degrees for 15-20 minutes, turning halfway.
4. NB: To maximize crispness, do not overcrowd the basket, rather fry in 2 batches but leave enough space in between the chicken to crisp to perfection.
5. Enjoy!

Air Fryer Chicken Cordon Bleu

Servings: 4

Cooking Time: 20 Minutes

Ingredients:

- 4 small chicken breasts boneless skinless, 4-5 oz each
- salt and ground black pepper to taste
- ⅛ teaspoon dried thyme leaves
- 4 slices deli Swiss cheese
- 4 slices deli ham
- 1 egg beaten
- ⅓ cup panko bread crumbs
- ½ cup seasoned bread crumbs

Directions:

1. Place the chicken breast on a flat work surface and butterfly the chicken by cutting most of the way through so it opens like a book. Pound to ¼ " thickness.
2. Season chicken with salt, pepper, and thyme.
3. Place the ham and cheese inside each chicken breast. Close the breasts and secure with a toothpick.
4. Mix panko bread crumbs and seasoned bread crumbs in a shallow dish. Dip chicken into egg and then bread crumbs.
5. Preheat the air fryer to 370°F.
6. Generously spray the rolls with cooking spray and place in the bottom of the air fryer basket.
7. Cook 10 minutes. Flip chicken over and cook an additional 8-10 minutes or until bread crumbs are crisp and chicken reaches 165°F.

Air-fryer Chicken Tenders

Servings: 4

Cooking Time: 15 Minutes

Ingredients:

- 1/2 cup panko bread crumbs
- 1/2 cup potato sticks, crushed
- 1/2 cup crushed cheese crackers
- 1/4 cup grated Parmesan cheese
- 2 bacon strips, cooked and crumbled
- 2 teaspoons minced fresh chives
- 1/4 cup butter, melted
- 1 tablespoon sour cream
- 1 pound chicken tenderloins
- Additional sour cream and chives

Directions:

1. Preheat air fryer to 400°. In a shallow bowl, combine the first 6 ingredients. In another shallow bowl, whisk butter and sour cream. Dip chicken in butter mixture, then in crumb mixture, patting to help coating adhere.
2. In batches, arrange chicken in a single layer on greased tray in air-fryer basket; spritz with cooking spray. Cook until coating is golden brown and chicken is no longer pink, 7-8 minutes on each side. Serve with additional sour cream and chives.

Air Fryer Whole Turkey With Gravy

Servings: 12

Cooking Time: 3 Hrs 15 Minutes

Ingredients:

- 14 lb. (6.35 kg) raw Whole Turkey
- 6 Tablespoons (90 g) butter , cut into slices
- 4 cloves garlic , sliced thin
- 1 Tablespoon (15 ml) kosher salt , or to taste
- black pepper , to taste
- Olive Oil (or oil of choice), to coat turkey
- 1 1/2 cups (360 ml) chicken broth
- 3/4 cup (95 g) all purpose flour (for the gravy)
- EQUIPMENT
- Halogen Air Fryer
- Instant Read Thermometer (optional)

Directions:

1. Thaw your turkey completely on the inside cavity. Remove and giblets and neck bones from the turkey cavity (many times the giblet pack will be tucked under the skin by the neck). Pat the turkey dry.
2. Tuck the butter slices and garlic in-between the skin and the turkey breasts. Rub olive oil over the turkey and season with salt and pepper.

3. Place the lower rack in the air fryer and spray with oil. Place the turkey breast side down in the air fryer. Pour in 1/2 cup of broth over the turkey. Place the extender ring and lid on the air fryer.
4. Air Fry the turkey at 350°F for about 2 1/2 to 3 hours.
5. Every 30 minutes, baste with chicken broth (the first 2 bastes will be with the remaining broth. After that, baste from the broth & juices at the bottom of the air fryer).
6. After cooking for 2 hours, take off the air fryer lid and extender ring. Lift the turkey out, flip to breast side up, and then place back into the air fryer. Baste the turkey and then place the extender ring and lid back on
7. Continue to Air Fry at 350°F until the turkey reaches an internal temperature of 165°F at the thickest parts of the thigh, wings and breast, and the juices run clear when you cut between the leg and the thigh (about 30 minutes - 1 hour).
8. Let rest for about 15-20 minutes.
9. While the turkey rests, make the gravy. Remove the lower rack from the air fryer. Leaving the turkey juices and broth in the air fryer, skim the chunks from the drippings and broth.
10. Place flour in a medium bowl. Ladle in about 1 cup of the drippings and broth into the flour and whisk until smooth. Pour the flour mixture into the air fryer with the remaining drippings and broth. Whisk until smooth.
11. Place the air fryer lid back on and Air Fry at 400°F for 10 minutes or until thickened, whisking a couple times while cooking.

Air-fryer Southern-style Chicken

Servings: 6
Cooking Time: 20 Minutes

Ingredients:
- 2 cups crushed Ritz crackers (about 50)
- 1 tablespoon minced fresh parsley
- 1 teaspoon garlic salt
- 1 teaspoon paprika

- 1/2 teaspoon pepper
- 1/4 teaspoon ground cumin
- 1/4 teaspoon rubbed sage
- 1 large egg, beaten
- 1 broiler/fryer chicken (3 to 4 pounds), cut up
- Cooking spray

Directions:
1. Preheat air fryer to 375°. In a shallow bowl, mix the first 7 ingredients. Place egg in a separate shallow bowl. Dip chicken in egg, then in cracker mixture, patting to help coating adhere. In batches, place chicken in a single layer on greased tray in air-fryer basket; spritz with cooking spray.
2. Cook 10 minutes. Turn chicken and spritz with cooking spray. Cook until chicken is golden brown and juices run clear, 10-20 minutes longer.

Air Fryer Chicken Strips

Servings: 8
Cooking Time: 12 Minutes

Ingredients:
- 1 1/2 lbs chicken breast skinless and boneless
- 2 cups all purpose flour I used half whole wheat
- 2 large eggs
- 2 cups panko bread crumbs
- 1/2 teaspoon salt
- 1/2 teaspoon pepper
- 1 teaspoon dehydrated garlic optional
- 1 tablespoon butter melted

Directions:
1. Preheat the air fryer to 200C/400F.
2. Pat dry the chicken breast and slice them into 2-inch strips.
3. In one bowl, add the flour, in another bowl, add the eggs, and in the third bowl, add the panko bread crumbs, salt, pepper, and garlic.
4. Moving quickly, dip the chicken in the flour, then the egg mix, then the panko mix. Shake off any excess.
5. Add the chicken strips to the greased air fryer basket. Brush the exterior of the chicken with some

butter and air fry for 12 minutes, flipping halfway through.

6. Once the chicken is cooked, remove it from the air fryer and serve immediately.

Notes

TO STORE: Leftovers can be stored in the refrigerator, covered, for up to five days.

TO FREEZE: Place the cooked and cooked breast strips in a shallow container and store them in the freezer for up to 6 months.

TO REHEAT: Either reheat back in the air fryer or a preheated oven. Avoid reheating in the microwave as the chicken will lose its crispiness.

Air Fryer Nashville Hot Chicken Hack

Servings: 2

Cooking Time: 20 Minutes

Ingredients:

- FOR THE CHICKEN:
- About 2-4 frozen pre-cooked breaded chicken breasts
- FOR THE NASHVILLE HOT SAUCE:
- 1/4 cup (60 g) butter
- 1/4 cup (60 ml) oil
- 1 Tablespoon (15 ml) ground cayenne pepper , or 2 Tablespoons for extra hot
- 2 Tablespoons (30 ml) brown sugar
- 1 teaspoon (5 ml) garlic powder
- 1 teaspoon (5 ml) paprika
- 1 Tablespoon (15 ml) Worcestershire sauce or soy sauce
- 1/2 teaspoon (2.5 ml) salt , or to taste
- 1 teaspoon (5 ml) black pepper
- FOR SERVING
- 6-8 slices (6-8 slices) white bread
- Pickles , whatever you prefer - bread & butter, dill, or both
- EQUIPMENT
- Air Fryer

Directions:

1. Make the Sauce: Combine all the sauce ingredients in a bowl or saucepan (butter, oil, cayenne pepper, brown sugar, garlic powder, paprika, Worcestershire or soy sauce, salt and pepper). Microwave or heat until butter is just melted (the hotter it is, the harder it will be to emulsify the spices in the liquids). Whisk thoroughly until smooth.

2. When the sauce is cooler, it doesn't separate as easily so we like to brush sauce on the chicken when the sauce is slightly cooler or room temperature. If you want your sauce warmer, then keep stirring or whisking the sauce as you brush the chicken so that you have as little separation of sauce/oil as possible. The warmer the sauce is, the more the spices will want to separate from the liquids.

3. Place the frozen breaded chicken breasts in the air fryer basket in a single layer. Make sure they aren't overlapping. No oil spray is needed.

4. Air Fry at 380°F/193°C for 10 minutes. Flip the chicken over.

5. Continue to Air Fry at 380°F/193°C for another 2 minutes. Check the chicken breasts and if needed, add another 2-3 minutes or until heated through and crispy to your preference.

6. Place chicken on top of white bread. Brush both sides of chicken with the hot sauce. Top with pickles and serve warm. Enjoy!

Notes

Air Frying Tips and Notes:

No Oil Necessary. Cook Frozen - Do not thaw first.

Don't overcrowd the air fryer basket. Lay in a single layer.

Recipe timing is based on a non-preheated air fryer. If cooking in multiple batches of chicken back to back, the following batches may cook a little quicker.

Recipes were tested in 3.7 to 6 qt. air fryers. If using a larger air fryer, the chicken might cook quicker so adjust cooking time.

Remember to set a timer to flip/toss as directed in recipe.

Dry Rubbed Wings With A Gorgonzola Dipping Sauce

Ingredients:

- WINGS:
- 4 lbs chicken wings
- 2 Tbsp vegetable oil1/2 Tbsp ancho chile pepper
- 1/2 Tbsp onion powder
- 1/2 Tbsp kosher salt
- 3/4 Tbsp light brown sugar, packed
- 3/4 tsp chili powder
- 3/4 tsp cumin
- 3/4 tsp paprika
- 1/2 tsp cayenne pepper
- 1/2 tsp dried mustard powder
- 1/2 tsp garlic powder
- 1/4 tsp black pepper
- 1/4 tsp dried oregano
- 1/4 tsp dried ground thyme
- GORGONZOLA DIPPING SAUCE:
- 1/2 cup mayonnaise
- 3 Tbsp buttermilk
- 1/4 cup sour cream
- 3 oz crumbled Gorgonzola cheese
- 1 clove garlic paste
- 1/4 tsp black pepper
- 1/4 tsp kosher salt

Directions:

1. Preheat the air fryer to 380°F degrees.
2. Combine all dry rub ingredients in a small mixing bowl and set aside.
3. In a large mixing bowl, add the chicken wings and vegetable oil and toss.
4. Sprinkle in about half of the dry rub mixture and toss the chicken wings to coat evenly. Note: This dry rub mixture is enough for 4 lbs of chicken wings, but feel free to use all the dry rub or save the remaining for later.
5. Remove the air fryer basket and spray with canola oil spray if desired. Add the chicken wings to the basket.
6. Set the timer to 30 minutes and utilizing the ALARM feature, select the 15 minute option to remind you to flip the wings halfway through.
7. While the wings are cooking, make the gorgonzola dipping sauce. Add the mayonnaise, buttermilk, sour cream, gorgonzola cheese, garlic, pepper and salt. Mix and refrigerate until it's time to serve.
8. Once the wings are done, serve immediately with the dipping sauce and carrot and celery sticks. Enjoy!

Air Fryer Sesame Chicken

Servings: 4

Cooking Time: 24 Minutes

Ingredients:

- Sauce Ingredients:
- 1/4 cup soy sauce
- 2 Tablespoons brown sugar
- 1 teaspoon orange zest
- 5 teaspoons Hoisin sauce
- 1/2 teaspoon ground ginger
- 1 teaspoon minced garlic
- 1 Tablespoon cold water
- 1 Tablespoon corn starch
- 2 teaspoons sesame seeds toasted
- Chicken Ingredients:
- 1 pound chicken thighs boneless skinless
- 1/3 cup corn starch
- 1 teaspoon olive oil spray

Directions:

1. Cut the chicken into cubed chunks, then toss in a large bowl with cornstarch and coat the chicken evenly.
2. Preheat the Air Fryer to 390° Fahrenheit.
3. Add the chicken to the prepared air fryer basket.
4. Air fry the chicken for 24 minutes until golden brown, tossing the chicken halfway through the cooking time. Add a spritz of oil after tossing the chicken.

5. Add the sesame chicken sauce ingredients into a small saucepan and whisk over medium heat until the sauce has reached a small boil.
6. Once the sugar has completely dissolved, whisk in the cornstarch and water. Allow the sauce to thicken for around 5 minutes. Continue to whisk.
7. Mix in the sesame seeds.
8. Remove the sauce from the heat and set aside for 5 minutes, allowing the sauce to continue thickening.
9. Place the chicken into a medium size mixing bowl and cover with the sauce. Toss the chicken so that each piece is coated in sauce.
10. Serve topped over rice and garnish with green onion.

Notes

Flour is a wonderful substitute for corn starch as it has starch in it already.

However, keep in mind; you will need twice as much flour as cornstarch to make

homemade sesame sauce.

You can also use chicken tenders or chicken breasts instead of chicken thighs.

Instead of corn starch, you can swap out tapioca flour to coat the chicken. You'll still

get crispy chicken without the added carbs.

Turkey Stuffed Air-fried Peppers

Servings: 3

Ingredients:
- 3 medium red sweet peppers
- 1 tablespoon olive oil
- 12 ounce ground turkey
- ½ cup cooked brown rice
- ¼ cup panko breadcrumbs
- ¾ cup low-sodium marinara sauce
- 3 tablespoon finely chopped flat-leaf parsley
- ¼ teaspoon ground pepper
- ¼ cup grated Parmesan cheese (1 oz.)
- ¼ cup shredded part-skim mozzarella cheese (1 oz.)

Directions:

1. Coat the basket of an air fryer with cooking spray. Cut tops off peppers and reserve. Seed the peppers and set aside.
2. Heat oil in a large skillet over medium-high heat. Add turkey; cook, stirring occasionally, until browned, about 4 minutes. Stir in rice and panko; cook, stirring occasionally, until warmed through, about 1 minute. Remove from heat and stir in marinara, parsley, pepper and Parmesan. Divide the mixture evenly among the prepared peppers.
3. Place the peppers in the prepared air-fryer basket. Nestle the pepper tops in the bottom of the basket. Cook at 350°F until the peppers are tender, about 8 minutes. Top with mozzarella; cook until the cheese is melted, about 2 minutes more.

Air Fryer Frozen Turkey Burgers

Servings: 4

Cooking Time: 15 Minutes

Ingredients:
- 4 frozen turkey burgers ½ inch thick
- 4 tablespoons barbecue sauce
- For Serving
- 4 hamburger buns
- lettuce, tomatoes, onions, mayonnaise optional

Directions:
1. Preheat air fryer to 375°F.
2. Place turkey burgers in a single layer in the air fryer basket.
3. Cook burgers for 13-14 minutes, flipping halfway through the cook time and brushing with bbq sauce.
4. Serve on hamburger buns with desired fixings.

Air Fryer Fried Chicken And Waffles

Servings: 4

Cooking Time: 30 Minutes

Ingredients:

- 8 chicken wings
- Chicken Seasoning or Chicken Rub
- pepper
- 1 tsp garlic powder
- 1 plastic bag
- 1/2 cup all-purpose flour
- cooking Oil
- 8 frozen waffles
- Maple Syrup (optional)

Directions:

1. In a medium bowl, season the chicken with the garlic powder and chicken seasoning and pepper to taste.
2. Transfer the chicken to a sealable plastic bag and add the flour. Shake to thoroughly coat the chicken.
3. Spray the air fryer basket with cooking oil.
4. Using tongs, transfer the chicken from the bag to the air fryer. It is okay to stack the chicken wings on top of each other. Spray them with cooking oil. Cook for 5 minutes.
5. Open the air fryer and shake the basket. Continue to cook the chicken. Repeat shaking every 5 minutes until 20 minutes has passed and the chicken is fully cooked.
6. Remove the cooked chicken from the air fryer and set aside.
7. Rinse the basket and base out with warm water. Return them to the air fryer.
8. Reduce the temperature of the air fryer to 370 degrees.
9. Place the frozen waffles in the air fryer. Do not stack. Depending on the size of your air fryer, you may need to cook the waffles in batches. Spray the waffles with cooking oil. Cook for 6 minutes.
10. If necessary, remove the cooked waffles from the air fryer, then repeat step 9 for the remaining waffles.
11. Serve the waffles with the chicken and a touch of maple syrup if desired.

Air Fryer 'kfc' Fried Chicken

Ingredients:

- Chicken:
- 8 pieces of free-range chicken – thighs and drumsticks (bone and skin on)
- 250ml buttermilk
- 1 free-range egg
- 1 Tbsp hot sauce (I use Cholula chipotle hot sauce)
- Flour coating:
- 2 cups flour
- 2 tsp salt
- 6 tsp dried herbs (thyme, sage, parsley, oregano, basil)
- 1 Tbsp celery salt
- 1 Tbsp fine white pepper powder (or a mix. Of black and white)
- 2 tsp Hot English mustard powder
- 1 Tbsp paprika
- 1 Tbsp garlic powder
- 2 tsp ground ginger
- Sunflower or canola oil for brushing / dabbing on the chicken

Directions:

1. Make the day before. Mix the buttermilk, egg, and hot sauce in a bowl and then add it to a Ziploc bag with the chicken. Seal and lay this flat in a dish overnight in the fridge.
2. Take the chicken out of the fridge at least an hour before you want to cook it so that it comes up to room temperature. Mix all the ingredients for the flour coating in a bowl until well combined.
3. Get a tray set out and lined with baking/silicone paper.
4. Dredge the chicken in the following order: Take the chicken from the buttermilk into the flour mixture

and toss to completely coat then set aside on the lined tray. You could dab/brush a little oil over the chicken at this stage and then proceed to the next step but first tossing it into the flour. Once all pieces are coated, quickly dip, and coat each piece 2 – 3 more times each. If some of the flour mixture clumps don't worry, try and press it onto the chicken.

5. Dab the top of each piece generously with olive oil. I used a silicone brush.

6. Preheat your Instant Vortex / Duo Crisp to 180C/350F. When it reaches temperature, spray the basket with non-stick cooking spray or olive oil / neutral oil spray. It's ok to use an aerosol spray if you have one. Or brush lightly with sunflower or canola oil.

7. Carefully place the chicken pieces in the basket and cook for 24 minutes. Turn them over halfway at 12 minutes. They should be golden brown and crunchy. Cook for a few extra minutes if you like them to be a darker colour. Serve with coleslaw or any other condiment of your choice.

Air Fryer Chicken Parmesan Recipe

Servings: 4
Cooking Time: 12 Minutes

Ingredients:

- 1/4 cup all-purpose flour
- 1/2 teaspoon garlic powder
- 1/2 teaspoon onion powder
- 1/2 cup panko breadcrumbs
- 2 ounces Parmesan cheese, grated (1 cup loosely packed or 1/2 cup store-bought)
- 2 large eggs
- 2 boneless, skinless chicken breasts (about 1 1/2 pounds total)
- 3/4 teaspoon kosher salt
- 1/4 teaspoon freshly ground black pepper
- Cooking spray
- 4 slices part-skim, low-moisture mozzarella cheese (about 4 ounces total)
- 1 cup store-bought or homemade marinara sauce

- Fresh basil leaves, for serving (optional)

Directions:

1. Place 1/4 cup all-purpose flour, 1/2 teaspoon garlic powder, and 1/2 teaspoon onion powder in a shallow bowl or plate and whisk to combine. Place 1/2 cup panko breadcrumbs and 2 ounces Parmesan cheese to a second shallow bowl or plate and whisk to combine. Add 2 large eggs to a third shallow bowl or plate and whisk to combine.

2. Slice 2 boneless, skinless chicken breasts in half horizontally (also known as butterflying). Season all over with 3/4 teaspoon kosher salt and 1/4 teaspoon black pepper.

3. Working with one piece of chicken at a time, coat the chicken in the flour mixture, then dip in the egg, letting any excess drip off. Coat in the panko-Parmesan crumbs. Place on a baking sheet or plate in a single layer.

4. Heat an air fryer to 400°F. Place 2 breaded chicken pieces in a single layer in the air fryer basket, making sure they do not overlap. Coat with cooking spray. Air fry until golden and crisp, 5 to 6 minutes.

5. Top each piece of chicken with a slice of mozzarella cheese, and secure each piece of cheese with 2 toothpicks. Air fry until the chicken is golden brown, an instant-read thermometer inserted into the center registers at least 165°F, and the cheese melts, 1 to 2 minutes more.

6. Transfer to a plate and cover loosely with aluminum foil. Repeat air frying the remaining chicken and cheese. When the second batch is almost ready, warm 1 cup marinara sauce on the stovetop over medium heat or in the microwave until warm.

7. To serve, remove the toothpicks, divide the marinara sauce evenly among serving plates, and nestle each serving of chicken Parmesan on top. Garnish with fresh basil leaves, if desired.

Recipe Notes

Storage: Refrigerate leftovers in an airtight container for up to 3 days.

Coronation Chicken

Servings: 2

Ingredients:

- 4 x 150g chicken breasts
- 1 tbsp oil
- 2 tsp curry paste
- 300g Greek yogurt
- 6 tbsp mayonnaise
- 1 tsp madras curry paste
- 2 tbsp mango chutney
- 50g dried apricots, chopped
- 100g pomegranate seeds
- 100g toasted pistachio nuts
- 25g flat leaf parsley, chopped, reserve some leaves to garnish
- Salt and freshly ground black pepper
- COOKING MODE
- When entering cooking mode - We will enable your screen to stay 'always on' to avoid any unnecessary interruptions whilst you cook!

Directions:

1. Brush chicken breasts with oil and curry paste.
2. Insert a crisper plate in Zone 1 drawer. Add chicken to Zone 1 drawer and insert into unit. Select Zone 1, turn the dial to select AIR FRY, set temperature to 200°C and set time to 16 minutes. Press the dial to begin cooking. Cooking is complete when the internal temperature reaches at least 75°C on an instant read thermometer.
3. Remove chicken from drawer and cut into chunks. Allow to cool.
4. In a small bowl, mix yogurt, mayonnaise, curry paste, chutney, apricot, pomegranate, pistachio seeds. Season to taste.
5. Delicious as a salad and can be used as a sandwich filler or served as a topping for a jacket potato.

Air Fryer Grilled Chicken Tenders

Servings: 4

Cooking Time: 10 Minutes

Ingredients:

- 10 chicken tenders
- 1 Tablespoon olive oil
- 1 teaspoon ground black pepper
- 1/2 teaspoon garlic powder
- 1/2 teaspoon onion powder
- 1/2 teaspoon paprika

Directions:

1. Preheat the Air Fryer to 400°F for 5 minutes. Prepare the Air Fryer basket with nonstick cooking spray or olive oil spray.
2. Using a cutting board, remove the tendon from the raw chicken tenders and add them to a medium-sized bowl.
3. Add the olive oil to the chicken tenders and toss them so that they are fully coated.
4. Add the seasonings to the chicken tenders and coat them.
5. Place the seasoned chicken in a single layer in the air fryer basket. Cook at 400°F for 10 minutes, flipping the chicken at the 5-minute mark. The chicken strips should be perfectly crispy and golden brown.
6. Use a meat thermometer to make sure the internal temperature reaches 165° degrees F. If not, cook for additional minutes until ready.
7. Serve the cooked chicken with your favorite dipping sauces, such as BBQ sauce, buffalo sauce, or honey mustard sauce.

Notes

It doesn't take long to cook these grilled chicken tenders in the air fryer with no breading. You should only need 15 minutes to have the most delicious and flavorful grilled chicken tenders.

To make your chicken tenders crispy, make sure you only use the recommended amount of oil or cooking spray. Using too much oil can make your chicken tenders greasy, and they won't crisp up.

You can store these easy chicken tenders in an airtight container for 3-4 days!

DESSERTS RECIPES

Roasted Pears & Shortbread

Servings: 6

Ingredients:

- For the shortbread
- 65g unsalted butter, room temperature
- 30g light brown soft or light muscovado sugar
- 75g plain flour
- 15g cornflour
- Pinch fine sea salt
- For the roasted pears
- 6 (approx. 150g each) conference pears
- 2 small lemons
- 1 small orange
- 80ml honey
- 15g unsalted butter
- 2 tbsp water
- To serve crème fraîche

Directions:

1. Cream the butter, sugar and salt together in a bowl for about one minute. Combine the plain flour and cornflour together well before adding to the creamed mixture and mixing to bring together. Chill
2. before using
3. Pat the mixture out onto a piece of baking parchment to a rectangle shape 16cm by 12cm. Place on a tray and chill for for 20-30 minutes, or until firm
4. Squeeze one of the lemons into a bowl and add enough cold water to eventually cover the pears. Peel the pears and place into the bowl as you go. With a peeler, peel 3-4 strips on both the remaining lemon and orange. Squeeze both and add the juice to a small saucepan along with the peel, honey, butter and 2 tablespoons of water. Heat to just dissolve the butter
5. When the shortbread dough is firm, prick all over with a fork and cut into 6 rough squares

6. Remove the crisper plates from both drawers. Arrange the pears lying down in the Zone 1 drawer. Pour all the juice and honey mixture over them then insert drawer in unit. Place the 6 shortbread biscuits in Zone 2 drawer, making sure to leave space around them then insert drawer in unit. There is no need to grease the drawer as the buttery biscuits won't stick!
7. Select Zone 1, turn the dial to select ROAST, set temperature to 190°C and set time to 40 minutes. Select Zone 2, turn the dial to select BAKE, set temperature to 150°C and set time to 35 minutes. Press the dial to begin cooking
8. Carefully give the pears a turn and baste 2 to 3 times whilst they are cooking. Check that they are tender with a knife or you can roast them for longer
9. Remove the shortbread from the drawer with help of a small plastic spatula and place them on a rack to cool. The cooking juices can be reduced in a saucepan to desired consistency if necessary. Serve the pears and shortbread with crème fraîche

Maple Roasted Acorn Squash

Servings: 4
Cooking Time: 15 Minutes

Ingredients:

- 1 acorn squash
- 1 tablespoon olive oil
- 2 tablespoons maple syrup
- 1/8 teaspoon coarse sea salt

Directions:

1. Preheat oven to 375 degrees (see below for air fryer directions).
2. Cut acorn squash in half and scoop out pulp and seeds.
3. Cut halves into 1-inch slices.
4. Spread oil on both side of slices and place on a baking sheet in a single even layer.
5. Baste maple syrup on top of each acorn squash slice.

6. Sprinkle sea salt on top evenly.
7. Bake for 15-20 minutes until fork pierces it easily.
8. Enjoy immediately or keep refrigerated for up to 3 days rcheating prior to serving.

Notes

Air Fryer Directions:

Prepare acorn squash as stated above.

Place slices in air fryer in a single layer.

Cook at 380 degrees for 10-12 minutes until easily pierced with a fork.

Air Fryer Biscuits

Servings: 8

Cooking Time: 9 Minutes

Ingredients:
- 2 cups self rising flour
- 1 cup buttermilk
- 1/2 cup butter frozen

Directions:
1. Preheat the air fryer to 180C/350F.
2. Sift the flour into a mixing bowl. Using a box grater, grate the frozen butter into the bowl.
3. Using your hands, gently mix the butter with the flour. Make a well in the center of the mixing bowl and add the buttermilk. Mix everything together.
4. Lightly flour a kitchen surface. Transfer the dough onto it. Gently knead it several times, then roll it flat. Knead and roll out several more times.
5. Using a biscuit cutter or large cookie cutter, push down in the dough and shape the biscuits.
6. Generously grease an air fryer basket. Add 4 biscuits to it, ensuring the sides are lightly touching.
7. Air fry the biscuits for 9-10 minutes, or until golden.
8. Remove the biscuits from the air fryer and repeat the process with the remaining biscuit dough.

Notes

TO STORE: Pack them in airtight containers to store at room temperature for up to 3 days. If you'd like them to keep longer, store them in the refrigerator for up to one week.

TO FREEZE: Place the cooked and cooled biscuits in a ziplock bag and store them in the freezer for up to 6 months.

Air-fryer Peaches With Vanilla-bean Ricotta

Servings: 4

Cooking Time: 15 Minutes

Ingredients:
- 4 yellow peaches, halved, destoned
- 1 tbs maple syrup
- 1 pinch ground cinnamon
- 1 cup light smooth ricotta
- 1/2 tsp vanilla-bean paste

Directions:
1. Place peaches in an air-fryer basket and brush with half of the maple syrup. Set temperature to 180°C and cook for 10 minutes or until peaches have softened.
2. Sprinkle with half of the cinnamon. Cook for a further 1 minute or until golden and caramelised.
3. Meanwhile, combine ricotta and vanilla in a small bowl.
4. Remove peaches from air fryer and drizzle with remaining maple syrup. Serve dolloped with ricotta mixture and sprinkled with remaining cinnamon.

Air-fryer Hot-cross-bun Ice-cream Balls

Servings: 4

Cooking Time: 10 Minutes

Ingredients:
- 500g vanilla ice-cream
- 1 pkt traditional hot cross buns
- 3 free range eggs
- 2 cups milk
- 5ml extra virgin olive oil cooking spray
- 1 cup caramel fudge topping
- 125g raspberries
- 2 bananas, sliced

Directions:

1. Line a baking tray with baking paper. Scoop ice-cream into 4 large walnut-sized balls. Place on tray and freeze for 2 hours or until very firm.

2. Roughly tear hot cross buns into pieces and then process until fine crumbs form.

3. Place on a large flat plate. Whisk eggs and milk in a large bowl.

4. Working quickly with one ball at a time, using 2 forks to hold ice-cream, dip in egg mixture then roll in hot-cross-bun crumbs to thickly coat, making sure ice-cream is completely covered in a thick layer of crumb. Then repeat to double crumb.

5. Place on tray and freeze for 4 hours or overnight until very firm.

6. Line basket of a 4L air fryer with baking paper. Spray ice-cream balls with cooking oil, then place in the air-fryer basket. Cook for 2-3 minutes on 200°C, or until golden brown and crisp. Carefully transfer balls to serving bowls. Drizzle with topping and serve with raspberries and banana.

Vortex Air Fryer Strawberry French Toast Bake

Servings: 8
Cooking Time: 25 Minutes

Ingredients:

- 4 teaspoons butter
- 1 pound loaf of brioche bread
- 8 eggs
- 2 cups milk
- 1 cup heavy cream
- 2 teaspoons vanilla extract
- 1 teaspoon cinnamon
- 8 ounces fresh strawberries cleaned and quartered
- 2 tablespoons brown sugar

Directions:

1. Find a baking dish that will fit in the Vortex. Cut or tear the brioche into chunks and place them in the baking dish.

2. In a large bowl whisk together eggs, milk, cream, vanilla, and cinnamon until well combined

3. Pour egg mixture over the bread, making sure all is coated

4. Cover the dish and cool in fridge overnight

5. Preheat your Air Fryer to 350°F on BAKE.

6. Tuck cut berries into the bread

7. Sprinkle on brown sugar and cover with tin foil

8. Bake for about 20 and then uncover and cook for 5-10 minutes or until golden brown and done in center

9. Serve with powdered sugar and/or syrup if desired

Zucchini Chocolate Chip Cookies

Servings: 2
Cooking Time: 10 Minutes

Ingredients:

- 1 1/2 c. all-purpose flour
- 1/4 tsp. kosher salt
- 1/4 tsp. baking soda
- 1/4 tsp. ground cinnamon
- 5 tbsp. butter, softened
- 1/2 c. granulated sugar
- 1/2 c. packed brown sugar
- 1 large egg
- 1/4 c. plain Greek yogurt
- 1 tsp. vanilla extract
- 1 c. shredded zuccini
- 1 c. semi-sweet chocolate chips
- 1 c. old-fashioned oats

Directions:

1. FOR OVEN

2. Preheat oven to 350°. In a small bowl, whisk together flour, salt, baking soda and cinnamon.

3. In a large bowl, beat together sugars and butter until light and fluffy. Add egg, yogurt, and vanilla and mix until evenly combined. Mix in flour mixture until just combined. Fold in oats, chocolate chips, and zucchini. Drop by rounded teaspoon 2 inches apart on baking sheets.

4. Bake for 15 minutes. Let cool for 2 minutes on baking sheet and transfer to wire rack to cool

completely. Note: Cookies will spread a bit, but not take on much color.

5. FOR AIR FRYER

6. In a small bowl, whisk together flour, salt, baking soda and cinnamon.

7. In a large bowl, beat together sugars and butter until light and fluffy. Add egg, yogurt, and vanilla and mix until evenly combined. Mix in flour mixture until just combined. Fold in oats, chocolate chips, and zucchini.

8. Line air fryer basket with parchment paper. Working in batches, use a small cookie scoop to scoop dough and place on parchment paper at least 1" apart.

9. Cook at 350° for 10 minutes?! Remove cookies and let cool on a wire rack, and repeat with remaining dough. Note: Cookies will not spread much, but will get golden brown.

Air Fryer Mint Aero Danish

Servings: 4

Cooking Time: 10 Minutes

Ingredients:

- 2 sheets frozen puff pastry, thawed
- 118g block Aero mint chocolate
- Thickened cream, to serve (optional)
- Select all Ingredients:

Directions:

1. Place 1 sheet of puff pastry on a flat working surface. Using an assortment of different-sized round cookie cutters, cut rounds from pastry, discarding trimmings.

2. Cut the remaining pastry sheet in half. Place the chocolate in the centre of 1 half of the pastry sheet. Brush the edges with a little cream and place the second half of the pastry sheet on top. Press the edges to seal. Brush with a little cream. Working with 1 pastry round at a time, place it over the top, pressing gently to secure to pastry. Repeat with remaining pastry rounds to form a decorative pattern. Trim pastry, leaving a 1cm border around chocolate.

3. Place in an air fryer and cook at 200C for 10 minutes or until crisp and golden. Turn air fryer off and let pastry sit for a further 5 minutes (this helps make the chocolate soft and gooey).

4. Cut into slices and serve with cream, if using.

Peppermint Cookies

Ingredients:

- 1/2 cup butter, softened
- 1/4 cup confectioners sugar
- 1/4 tsp peppermint extract
- 1/2 cup + 2 Tbsp flour
- 1/4 cup cornstarch
- 1 cup vanilla frosting, store bought or homemade
- Red food coloring
- Peppermint candies, crushed

Directions:

1. Preheat your air fryer oven to 350°F.

2. In a mixing bowl, add the softened butter, confectioners sugar and peppermint extract and mix. Set aside.

3. In another bowl, whisk together the flour and cornstarch.

4. Next, add in the wet ingredients in with the dry ingredients. This will make a crumbly dough.

5. Refrigerate for about 30 minutes.

6. Grease the air fryer's baking sheet.

7. Remove the dough from the refrigerator and roll into 6 regular sized cookie balls or about 8-10 small cookies.

8. Bake for 10 minutes then cool on a rack for at least 10 minutes.

9. Take your 1 cup of frosting and combine 1-2 drops of red food coloring to make a subtle reddish, pinky color.

10. Put the peppermint candies in a baggy and crush.

11. Frost the tops of each cookie and sprinkle with the crushed peppermint candies!

Air Fryer Chocolate Croissants

Servings: 8

Cooking Time: 7 Minutes

Ingredients:

- 1 can Crescent Roll Dough
- 8 mini Chocolate Bars or ½ cup chocolate chips

Directions:

1. Unroll the crescent roll sheet and then dividing into triangles.
2. Place one piece of chocolate, or one tablespoon of chocolate chip, at the end of the crescent roll and roll until into a crescent shape.
3. Spray the air fryer basket or baking sheet with non-stick cooking spray or line basket with parchment paper. Place croissants in the prepared basket, leaving a small space between each pastry.
4. Air fry at 350 degrees Fahrenheit for about 5-7 minutes until crescent rolls are golden brown.
5. Carefully remove filled chocolate crescent rolls from the Air Fryer. Sprinkle each puff pastry with powdered sugar, slices of almonds, drizzle with chocolate syrup or frosting glaze.

Notes

I make these in my Cosori 5.8 Air Fryer Model. Depending on the size and wattage of the Air Fryer, you may need to add an additional 1-2 minutes to cook time.

Leave enough room between each pastry, allowing room for the roll to puff as it cooks.

Do not stack or overlap in the basket. The dough may not cook evenly.

You can make 4 or 8 in a batch, depending on what will fit in your basket.

Frozen Grands Biscuits In Air Fryer

Servings: 6

Cooking Time: 22 Minutes

Ingredients:

- 6 Frozen Grands Biscuits
- oil spray
- butter and/or jam , optional

Directions:

1. Spray the air fryer basket or racks with oil to keep the biscuits from sticking. We don't suggest using parchment paper underneath because you want maximum air flow under the biscuits to help them cook all the way though. The parchment paper prevents maximum air flow under the biscuits.
2. Lay biscuits in single layer of air fryer basket or racks. Make sure to space them out so they aren't touching & have room to rise & expand. Cook in batches if needed.
3. Spray the tops of the biscuits to give them a more golden top when they air fry.
4. Air Fry at 330°F/165°C for 10 minutes. Gently wiggle the biscuits to loosen from the baskets. Flip the biscuits over.
5. Continue to Air Fry at 330°F/165°C for another 8-12 minutes, or until golden and cooked through. If they're still slightly doughy in the middle, leave them in the turned-off air fryer for about 2-3 minutes to continue cooking in the residual heat. Serve with butter or jam if desired.

Gingerbread Cookies In The Air Fryer

Servings: 12

Cooking Time: 8 Minutes

Ingredients:

- 2 3/4 cups all-purpose flour
- 1 tsp baking soda
- ½ tsp ground cinnamon
- ½ tsp ground nutmeg
- 1/2 tsp ground ginger
- ½ tsp salt
- 1/2 cup butter softened
- 3/4 cup brown sugar
- 1 egg large
- ⅓ cup molasses
- 1 teaspoon vanilla

Directions:

1. In a medium bowl, combine the flour, baking soda, ginger, cinnamon, nutmeg, and salt in a bowl, then set the bowl aside.
2. In a large bowl, or stand mixer, add the butter and sugar. Beat together at medium speed. Add in the egg, vanilla, and molasses. Continue mixing on medium speed until well combined.
3. Slowly, add in the flour mixture, and continue mixing until all ingredients are combined. Scrape the inside of the bowl if needed.
4. Wrap and chill dough for about 30 minutes.
5. On a lightly floured surface, roll the dough about ¼ inch in thickness. Use cookie cutters to cut into your favorite shapes.
6. Place cookies in the air fryer basket, lined with parchment paper.
7. Air fry at 350 degrees F for 8-10 minutes until dough is cooked.
8. Allow cookies to cool for 2-3 minutes before removing from the air fryer basket. Then transfer cookies to a wire rack to cool completely.

Notes

The great thing about these ginger molasses cookies is that you can use the cookie dough for making fun edible things! Grab some cookie cutters and make shapes besides gingerbread men, or even divide dough so that you can create gingerbread houses as well.

Once you bake cookies, you can decorate the gingerbread people and use royal icing from a pastry bag and create an epic gingerbread man! (or decorate those gingerbread houses!)

Air Fryer Caramelized Bananas

Servings: 4

Cooking Time: 10 Minutes

Ingredients:

- 2 large bananas, peeled and cut into 1/2 inch slices
- 1 tablespoon salted butter, melted
- 1/2 teaspoon vanilla extract
- 1 tablespoon brown sugar
- 1/2 teaspoon ground cinnamon

Directions:

1. Preheat air fryer to 390 degrees F (195 degrees C)
2. Spread out banana slices on a plate. Combine butter and vanilla extract and drizzle over the bananas.
3. Combine brown sugar and cinnamon. Sprinkle half of the sugar mixture over the slices, flip, and sprinkle the remaining sugar over the other side. Make sure both sides are well coated.
4. Spray the air fryer basket with cooking spray or line with a parchment paper.
5. Place banana slices in the air fryer basket in a single layer
6. making sure not to overcrowd or overlap. Cook until golden brown and caramelized to your liking, 7 to 9 minutes. You do not need to flip banana slices over.
7. Remove bananas from the basket, cool slightly, and serve.

Notes

Depending on the size of your air fryer you may need to fry bananas in batches.

Cooking time may vary depending on the size and brand of your air fryer. If you are only have unsalted butter, add a pinch of salt.

Vegetable Fritters

Servings: 6

Cooking Time: 25 Minutes

Ingredients:

- 1 large (375 g) zucchini
- 2 medium (300 g) potatoes (Yukon Gold or Russet)
- 1 medium (80 g) carrot
- ½ tsp garlic powder
- ½ tsp onion powder
- ½ tsp chili powder
- ½ tsp ground cumin
- ½ tsp paprika powder
- ½ tsp sea salt
- Black pepper to taste
- ½ cup (50 g) chickpea flour

Directions:

1. You can watch the short video for visual instructions.
2. Grate the zucchini, potatoes, and carrot. Then squeeze out as much liquid as possible using a nut-milk bag, cheesecloth, or a clean kitchen towel.
3. Add the veggies to a skillet and stir in all spices. Cook the veggies over low-medium heat with a lid for about 10 minutes, stirring occasionally, then turn off the heat.
4. Add in the chickpea flour and stir with a spatula to combine. Let the mixture cool, until you can touch it.
5. Shape the mixture into 6 patties, using your hands. You can choose between the following three cooking methods:
6. Air-Fry
7. Cook at 380 °F (195 °C) for 15 minutes in your air fryer (flip after 10 minutes). I recommend spraying the basket of your air fryer with a little oil before adding the patties, otherwise, they may stick.
8. Pan-Fry
9. Heat some oil in a frying pan and place 3-4 patties in it. Fry on both sides until crispy (about 4-5 minutes per side).
10. Bake
11. Preheat the oven to 400 °F (205 °C) and bake the patties for 35-40 minutes on a lined baking sheet (flipping after 20-25 minutes). For a crispier result, I recommend spraying the patties with a little oil before baking and after flipping.
12. Enjoy with a dip of choice, e.g. this vegan ranch dressing.

Notes

Find 40 more vegan air-fryer recipes in the blog post above.

Cherry Hand Pies

Servings: 14

Cooking Time: 8 Minutes

Ingredients:

- Cherry Hand Pie:
- 12 ounces frozen or fresh cherries, pitted
- 1 tablespoon lemon juice
- ¼ cup granulated sugar
- A pinch of kosher salt
- 1 tablespoon cornstarch
- ½ teaspoon almond extract
- 2 sheets frozen puff pastry, thawed
- 1 egg, beaten
- Glaze:
- 1 cup powdered sugar
- 1 tablespoon whole milk
- ½ teaspoon vanilla extract
- Items Needed:
- Rolling pin
- 3-inch round cutter
- Baking sheet
- Wax paper

Directions:

1. Combine the cherries, lemon juice, sugar, and salt in a saucepan over medium-high heat. Bring mixture to a boil, then reduce to a simmer for 5 minutes.
2. Smash some of the cherries lightly with a fork.

3. Place the cornstarch in a small bowl. Add 3 tablespoons of the cherry liquid and stir until no clumps remain.

4. Pour the cornstarch mixture into the saucepan and stir. When the mixture thickens, remove from heat, stir in the almond extract, and refrigerate until slightly chilled.

5. Roll out each puff pastry sheet on a floured surface into a 9 x 12-inch rectangle. Using a 3-inch round cutter, cut out circles in the puff pastry.

6. Place the circles onto a baking sheet lined with wax paper.

7. Spoon about 2 teaspoons of cherry filling onto half of the puff pastry circles. Brush the edges with some of the beaten egg and place the remaining puff pastry circles on top to enclose.

8. Press the edges with a fork to seal. Refrigerate for 20 minutes.

9. Select the Preheat function on the Air Fryer, adjust temperature to 350°F, and press Start/Pause.

10. Cut a 1-inch vent in the top of each pastry. Brush the tops with more of the beaten egg.

11. Place the cherry hand pies into the preheated fryer baskets.

12. Set time to 8 minutes, then press Start/Pause.

13. Remove when golden and puffed. Transfer to a wire rack immediately and allow to cool completely.

14. Whisk the glaze ingredients together in a small bowl until smooth, then glaze the cooled cherry hand pies.

15. Serve the pies when the glaze is set.

Air Fryer Halloumi Cheese

Servings: 12

Cooking Time: 7 Minutes

Ingredients:

- 8 ounces halloumi cheese
- 2 teaspoons olive oil
- cooking spray

Directions:

1. Preheat the air fryer to 360 degrees F (180 degrees C).

2. Slice halloumi into 6 equal slices, cut each slice in half, and dry with a paper towel. Brush all sides with olive oil.

3. Lightly spray the air fryer basket with cooking spray. Place the halloumi slices in the basket, making sure they're not touching. You may have to cook in two batches,

4. Cook for 7 to 9 minutes until golden brown, but make sure not to overcook or they turn rubbery. Serve immediately.

Notes

Cooking time may vary depending on the brand and size of your air fryer.

Cranberry Apple Crisp

Servings: 6-8

Cooking Time: 30 Minutes

Ingredients:

- Filling:
- 1½ cups fresh cranberries
- 2 Granny Smith apples, cut into 1-inch cubes
- 2 Gala apples (Fuji or Pink Lady), cut into 1-inch cubes
- ¼ cup maple syrup
- 3 tablespoons brown sugar
- 1 tablespoon cane sugar
- ½ teaspoon cinnamon
- ½ teaspoon allspice
- ½ teaspoon lemon juice
- 2 tablespoons cornstarch
- ¼ teaspoon salt
- Oil spray
- Topping:
- 1½ cups rolled oats
- ⅓ cup brown sugar
- 4 tablespoons flour
- 4 tablespoons coconut oil, melted
- ¼ teaspoon cinnamon
- A pinch of salt
- Non-dairy or low-calorie ice cream, for serving (optional)

Directions:

1. Combine all the ingredients for the filling except the oil spray in a large bowl and set aside.
2. Mix the ingredients for the toppings thoroughly in a separate medium bowl.
3. Coat the Smart Air Fryer basket with oil spray.
4. Pour the filling mixture directly into the air fryer basket, without the crisper plate. Spread the mixture evenly.
5. Sprinkle the topping across the top of the filling mixture.
6. Select the Bake function, adjust temperature to 325°F and time to 30 minutes, then press Start/Pause.
7. Remove the cranberry apple crisp when done and serve warm with your choice of ice cream.

Air Fryer Gingersnap Cookies

Servings: 12
Cooking Time: 6 Minutes

Ingredients:

- 1 cup all-purpose flour
- 1/2 cup brown sugar packed
- 1/3 cup butter softened
- 2 tablespoons molasses
- 1 large egg
- 1/2 teaspoon baking soda
- 1/2 teaspoon ground ginger
- Cinnamon Sugar Topping
- 1/4 cup granulated sugar
- 1 tablespoon ground cinnamon

Directions:

1. In a small shallow bowl or flat plate, combine the sugar and cinnamon for the topping. Stir dry ingredients together and set aside.
2. In a medium bowl, cream butter with brown sugar. Add in molasses, egg, baking soda, and ground ginger. Mix on medium speed until mixture becomes thick and creamy.
3. Slowly begin to add in flour (about a ¼ cup at a time). Continue to mix together until a soft dough

forms. Make sure all flour from sides of bowl have been fully incorporated into the dough mixture.

4. Use a cookie scoop or spoon shape dough into small balls (about 1-1 ½ inches in size). Roll them in cinnamon sugar mixture and set aside on a baking sheet until all dough has been used.
5. Line your air fryer with parchment paper and place balls in a single layer. Leave enough room between cookies to slightly spread as they cook. Air fry at 320 degrees F for 6-8 minutes.
6. Allow cookies to cool before removing them from your air fryer basket. If you are making a couple of batches, you can remove cookies when slightly warm and let them finish cooling on a wire rack.

Notes

Optional flavors: Adding a pinch pumpkin pie spice, nutmeg and clove will boost the ginger taste. Creating a family favorite warm spice mixture makes them extra special.

Optional drinks to go with this chewy cookie: Dunking them into a warm cup of tea, a glass of cold milk, a hot toddy or your favorite morning brewed coffee on a cold winter's day are always yummy.

Peanut Butter Banana Oat Protein Cookies

Servings: 4
Cooking Time: 20 Minutes

Ingredients:

- 2 medium very ripe bananas
- 1 cup old fashioned oats (or quick oats (check labels for gluten-free))
- 1 scoop vanilla protein powder (I like Orgain)
- 1 large egg (lightly beaten)
- ¼ teaspoon cinnamon
- Pinch kosher salt
- ½ teaspoon vanilla extract
- ¼ cup peanut butter (or nut butter, or seed butter)
- ¼ cup sugar free chocolate chips (such as Lily's)

Directions:

1. Preheat oven to 350 degrees F. Line 2 sheet pans with parchment or silicon baking mats.
2. Move oven racks to the second from top and second from bottom slots.
3. In a medium bowl, mash the bananas.
4. Add the oats, protein powder, egg, cinnamon, salt, vanilla, and peanut butter and chocolate chips and mix with a fork until combined.
5. Scoop ¼ cup of mixture and place on a baking sheet, flatten the top slightly with the back of the measuring cup. Repeat with remaining mixture, adding 4 cookies to each sheet.
6. Bake for 16 to 20 minutes, rotating pans ½ through bake time to allow for even browning.
7. Allow to cool 5 minutes on the pan then transfer to a wire rack to cool completely.

Notes

Store in an airtight container in the refrigerator for up to 4 days. Can be eaten warm, cold, at room temperature or warmed in the microwave for 10 seconds.

Air Fryer Brownies

Servings: 2
Cooking Time: 15 Minutes

Ingredients:

- 1/4 cup All-Purpose Flour
- 3/4 cup Semi-sweet chocolate **chopped finely, 85 g. Buy the best quality you can afford.
- 2 tbsp Cocoa Powder
- 1/3 cup white sugar **if you prefer more sweet add ½ cup
- 1/4 tsp Baking Powder
- Kosher Salt **a pinch. Or you can use regular salt.
- 1/2 tsp Vanilla Extract
- 1 large egg. **room temperature
- 1/4 cup Unsalted Butter **melted and cooled slightly
- 2 tbsp Semi-sweet chocolate **chopped roughly.

Directions:

1. Begin by melting the finely chopped chocolate in a completely dry microwave safe bowl in the microwave oven in 10 seconds bursts. Stir in between. Do this until the chocolate is completely melted. It'll look silky smooth & shiny. Set it aside.
2. Mix the sugar and melted butter together until just combined. You can use a hand whisk or a fork to do the job.
3. Crack a room temperature egg and whisk to mix it with the sugar butter mixture. Whisk until the egg is uniformly combined.
4. Now, add the vanilla extract and give the wet ingredients a quick stir.
5. In a separate bowl whisk together all the dry ingredients (until just combined) like the flour, cocoa powder, salt & the baking powder. Use a fork or a hand whisk.
6. Now, add the dry ingredients to the wet ingredients and mix well with the help of a spatula until combined. Avoid over mixing.
7. Add the melted chocolate and gently fold it in into the brownie batter with the help of a spatula.
8. Now, for a super fudgy and moist brownie add in the roughly chopped chocolate and gently fold it in the brownie batter. The batter is ready.
9. Place the air fryer basket inside the steel insert of the Instant Pot (make sure the Instant pot is unplugged) and place the perforated metal disc inside the air fryer basket.
10. Line a 6 inch cake mold with parchment paper (makes it so easy to take out the brownie without breaking it).
11. Transfer the brownie batter into the parchment layered cake pan. Try to spread it evenly with the help of a spatula as much as you can (it's a super thick batter).
12. Place the cake pan on the perforated metal disc inside the air fryer basket.
13. Secure the Air Fryer lid and plug it in. Hit the Air Fryer button and Air Fry at 350 degrees F for 15 minutes.
14. Once, the cooking cycle is over the Instant Pot will begin to beep. Hit the CANCEL button and open the air fryer lid carefully and place it on top of the

heat proof lid base (comes along with the air fryer lid).

15. Insert a tooth pick at the center of the brownie to check the doneness. The toothpick must not come out clean.

16. Bring out the cake pan and place it on top of the kitchen counter and allow it to rest for at least 30 minutes or until the brownie have come down to the room temperature.

17. Grab the ends of the parchment paper and carefully bring out the brownie. Slice and serve with vanilla ice-cream. Enjoy!

Notes

Sugar: You can use ½ cup sugar to make the brownie if you prefer very sweet desserts. We used ⅓ cup sugar.

Chopped Chocolate: Use the best quality chocolate you can afford. The better the quality of the chocolate the fudgier and tastier the brownie would be. I used 70% semi-sweet organic chocolate slabs.

Melting the Chopped chocolate: The melted chocolate will make the interior of the brownie incredibly moist, fudgy and chocolaty. Your brownies will be outstanding. Don't skip the chocolate and always melt it in completely dry microwave safe bowl. A single drop of water will seize the chocolate and it will be lumpy and grainy instead of silky, smooth and shiny.

DO NOT change any ingredient quantities.

Brownie consistency: Fudgy & chewy with a crackly top.

Storing Tips: The Brownie will last in the fridge for 7 days. They will become hard as it contains butter. Allow the brownies to come down to room temperature or just warm them up slightly in the microwave oven before serving.

Serving Ideas: Serve these insanely fudgy air fryer brownies with vanilla ice-cream or milk. So yum!

Can you freeze the Air fryer brownies? I would not recommend freezing the air fryer brownies because the consistency and texture of the brownie would change. It's a small batch brownie and would be gone fast :D

Air Fryer Oatmeal Cookies

Servings: 24

Cooking Time: 9 Minutes

Ingredients:

- ½ cup butter softened
- ¼ cup sugar
- ½ cup packed brown sugar
- 1 egg large, room temperature
- ½ teaspoon vanilla
- 1 ½ cups quick-cooking oats
- ¾ cup all-purpose flour + 2 tablespoons
- ½ teaspoon baking soda
- 1 teaspoon salt
- ½ teaspoon cinnamon
- ½ cup chocolate chips
- ½ cup raisins

Directions:

1. Preheat air fryer to 325°F without parchment paper.

2. Cream butter and sugar in a bowl with a hand mixer. Beat in egg and vanilla.

3. Combine oats, flour, baking soda, cinnamon, and salt in a bowl. Add a bit at a time to the egg mixture.

4. Fold in chocolate chips and raisins.

5. Place tablespoons of cookie dough on a small piece of parchment paper in the air fryer basket about 1" apart.

6. Air fry for 6-9 minutes or just until golden on the edges. Repeat with remaining dough, subsequent batches may take 1 minute less.

Notes

For high-rising cookies, avoid overmixing the dough.

Chill the dough for 30 minutes before air frying so the cookies spread evenly.

Key Lime Pie

Servings: 6

Cooking Time: 20 Minutes

Ingredients:

- 6 graham crackers
- 3 tablespoons unsalted butter, melted
- 1 tablespoon granulated sugar
- 4 large egg yolks
- 1 can sweetened condensed milk
- ½ cup key lime juice
- 1/3 cup creme fraiche
- 1 tablespoon lime zest
- 1 teaspoon vanilla extract
- Toppings
- ½ cup heavy whipping cream
- 2 tablespoons powdered sugar
- Items Needed:
- Food processor
- 7-inch springform pan
- Metal rack accessory

Directions:

1. Place the graham crackers in the bowl of a food processor fitted with the blade attachment, then blend until the crackers are broken down into crumbs.
2. Pour the crumbs into a bowl and mix with the granulated sugar and melted butter. Press the mixture into the bottom of a 7-inch springform pan, then freeze for 20 minutes.
3. Whisk the egg yolks until they have turned a light shade of yellow, then whisk in the condensed milk until the mixture is thickened. Gradually whisk in the key lime juice, crème fraiche, lime zest, and vanilla extract.
4. Remove the springform pan from the freezer and pour the pie filling over the crust.
5. Pour 1 ½ cups of water into the inner pot of the pressure cooker and place the metal rack accessory into the pot, then place the springform pan onto the rack.

6. Place the lid onto the pressure cooker and slide the vent switch to Seal.
7. Select the Pressure Cook function and press Keep Warm to disable.
8. Adjust pressure to high and time to 15 minutes, then press Start.
9. Release pressure naturally for 5 minutes by leaving the pressure cooker alone, then slide the vent switch to Vent to quickly release the remaining pressure.
10. Open the lid carefully and lift the rack out of the inner pot, then let the pie cool to room temperature before placing it in the refrigerator to chill for at least 6 hours.
11. Beat the whipped cream and powdered sugar to stiff peaks and reserve for a garnish.
12. Serve the key lime pie cold, cut into wedges, garnished with dollops of whipped cream.

Air Fryer Donuts

Servings: 12

Cooking Time: 4 Minutes

Ingredients:

- 1 cup milk lukewarm (about 100°F)°
- 2 1/2 tsp active dry yeast or instant yeast
- 1/4 cup granulated sugar plus 1 tsp
- 1/2 tsp salt
- 1 egg
- 1/4 cup unsalted butter melted
- 3 cups all-purpose flour
- Oil Spray Coconut oil works best
- For the Glaze
- 6 Tbsp unsalted butter
- 2 cups powdered sugar
- 2 tsp vanilla extract
- 4 Tbsp hot water or as needed

Directions:

1. In the bowl of a stand mixer fitted with the dough hook, gently stir together lukewarm milk, 1 tsp of sugar, and yeast. Let it sit for 10 minutes until

foamy (If nothing happens your milk was too hot or the yeast is too old, so start over).

2. Add sugar, salt, egg, melted butter and 2 cups of flour to the milk mixture. Mix on low speed until combined, then with the mixer running add the remaining cup of flour slowly, until the dough no longer sticks to the bowl. Increase speed to medium-low and knead for 5 minutes, until the dough is elastic and smooth.

3. Place the dough into a greased bowl and cover it with plastic wrap. Let rise in a warm place until doubled. Dough is ready if you make a dent with your finger and the indention remains.

4. Turn the dough out onto a floured surface, punch it down and gently roll out to about 1/2 inch thickness. Cut out 10-12 donuts using a 3-inch round cutter and a 1-inch round cutter to remove center.

5. Transfer donuts and donut holes to lightly floured parchment paper and cover loosely with greased plastic wrap. Let donuts rise until doubled in volume, about 30 minutes. Preheat Air Fryer to 350F.

6. Spray Air Fryer basket with oil spray, carefully transfer donuts to Air Fryer basket in a single layer. Spray donuts with oil spray and cook at 350F until golden brown, about 4 minutes. Repeat with remaining donuts and holes.

7. While the donuts are in the Air Fryer, melt butter in a small saucepan over medium heat. Stir in powdered sugar and vanilla extract until smooth. Remove from heat and stir in hot water one tablespoon at a time until the icing is somewhat thin, but not watery. Set aside.

8. Dip hot donuts and donut holes in the glaze using to forks to submerge them. Place on a wire rack set over a rimmed baking sheet to allow excess glaze to drip off. Let sit until glaze hardens, about 10 minutes.

Notes

Make sure the milk is not hotter than 115 degrees F. Using hot liquid will kill the yeast.

If you don't have an instant read thermometer, drizzle a few drops of the warmed up milk onto the inside of your wrist. It should feel warm. If it feels hot the yeast will die off, if it feels cold it will remain dormant.

BREAKFAST & BRUNCH RECIPES

Air Fryer Garlic Bread

Servings: 4
Cooking Time: 6 Minutes

Ingredients:

- Half loaf of bread
- 3 tablespoons butter, softened
- 3 garlic cloves, minced
- 1/2 teaspoon dried Italian seasoning
- small pinch of red pepper flakes

Directions:

1. Preheat your air fryer to 350 degrees.
2. Cut the bread in half or sized to fit your air fryer.
3. Mix the butter, garlic, Italian seasoning, and red pepper flakes in a small bowl.
4. Baste the garlic butter mixture on top of the bread evenly.
5. Place the garlic bread in the air fryer side by side and cook for 6 to 7 minutes until browned to your liking.

Air Fryer Hard Boiled Eggs

Servings: 6
Cooking Time: 15 Minutes

Ingredients:

- 6 large eggs

Directions:

1. Place baking rack in the bowl in the low position. Carefully place eggs on top.
2. Tap the bake button and set temperature to 300°F and fry for 12-14 minutes.
3. Note: 12 minutes for a looser yolk. 14 minutes for a set yolk.
4. Carefully move eggs, with tongs, to a bowl of cold water for 5-10 minutes.
5. Tap eggs on a hard surface and peel.
6. Store in an airtight container in the refrigerator for 3-4 days.

Air Fryer Frozen Burritos

Servings: 4
Cooking Time: 10 Minutes

Ingredients:

- 4 burritos frozen

Directions:

1. Preheat your Air Fryer to 400 degrees Fahrenheit or 200 degrees Celcius. Prepare the air fryer basket.
2. Place the frozen burritos in air fryer basket.
3. Air fry at the frozen burritos at 400 degrees Fahrenheit for 12-15 minutes. Make sure to flip the burritos several times during the cooking process.

Notes

What toppings go well with burritos?

Literally, anything that you're wanting. I love to add a bit of hot sauce to the outside of the crispy tortilla and I really make sure to over the outside of the burrito with sour cream and chives as well.

Don't forget to top with a bit of lime juice as well!

Air Fryer Bacon And Egg Breakfast Biscuit Bombs

Servings: 10

Ingredients:

- Biscuit Bombs
- 4 slices bacon, cut into 1/2-inch pieces
- 1 tablespoon butter·
- 2 eggs, beaten
- 1/4 teaspoon pepper
- 1 can (10.2 oz) refrigerated Pillsbury™ Grands!™ Southern Homestyle Buttermilk Biscuits (5 Count)
- 2 oz sharp cheddar cheese, cut into ten 3/4-inch cubes
- Egg Wash
- 1 egg
- 1 tablespoon water

Directions:

1. Cut two 8-inch rounds of cooking parchment paper. Place one round in bottom of air fryer basket. Spray with cooking spray.

2. In 10-inch nonstick skillet, cook bacon over medium-high heat until crisp. Remove from pan; place on paper towel. Carefully wipe skillet with paper towel. Add butter to skillet; melt over medium heat. Add 2 beaten eggs and pepper to skillet; cook until eggs are thickened but still moist, stirring frequently. Remove from heat; stir in bacon. Cool 5 minutes.

3. Meanwhile, separate dough into 5 biscuits; separate each biscuit into 2 layers. Press each into 4-inch round. Spoon 1 heaping tablespoonful egg mixture onto center of each round. Top with one piece of the cheese. Gently fold edges up and over filling; pinch to seal. In small bowl, beat remaining egg and water. Brush biscuits on all sides with egg wash.

4. Place 5 of the biscuit bombs, seam sides down, on parchment in air fryer basket. Spray both sides of second parchment round with cooking spray. Top biscuit bombs in basket with second parchment round, then top with remaining 5 biscuit bombs.

5. Set to 325°F; cook 8 minutes. Remove top parchment round; using tongs, carefully turn biscuits, and place in basket in single layer. Cook 4 to 6 minutes longer or until cooked through (at least 165°F).

Air Fryer Churros

Servings: 6
Cooking Time: 8 Minutes

Ingredients:

- 3/4 cup water
- 1/4 cup butter cut into cubes (4 tbs)
- 1 tablespoon sugar
- 1/2 teaspoon salt
- 1/2 teaspoon ground cinnamon
- 1 cup all purpose flour plus 1-2 tablespoons
- 2 large eggs
- Cinnamon Sugar
- 1/2 cup sugar

- 1 tablespoon ground cinnamon

Directions:

1. In a medium saucepan, add water, butter, sugar, and salt. Heat on medium to high heat until it begins to boil. Stir continuously until butter has melted and sugar and salt are dissolved. Let boil for at least 2-3 minutes.

2. Remove from heat and let mixture cool for about 30 seconds, then add in flour and cinnamon. Then beat in whisked eggs. If dough is too sticky, add in 1-2 extra tablespoons of flour. Dough will be slightly sticky but thick enough to hold shape.

3. Transfer dough to a piping bag with a large star tip. (I use 1M tip)

4. Pipe dough onto baking sheet lined with air fryer parchment paper, into 4-6 inch strips, then place baking sheet in the refrigerator to chill for 30-45 minutes, or freezer for 15 minutes, until dough is firm.

5. Gently transfer parchment paper with piped dough into the air fryer basket. Air fry at 350 degrees for 8-10 minutes, until golden brown.

6. Combine sugar and cinnamon in a small bowl. Brush churros with melted butter, then toss churros with sugar mixture until well coated.

Notes

Optional Ingredients: You can dust the churros with powdered sugar, or brown sugar with fall spices. They can also be stuffed with Nutella, peanut butter and jelly, or vanilla pudding.

Kitchen Tips: If you do not have piping bags no worries a resealable plastic bag works just as well. Use a pair of kitchen shears or kitchen scissors to cut one small corner of bag to desired thickness before piping out dough. You can use an electric hand mixer instead of stirring on stovetop if you prefer.

Frozen Egg Rolls In The Air Fryer

Servings: 5

Cooking Time: 8 Minutes

Ingredients:

- 5 frozen egg rolls

Directions:

1. Preheat your air fryer to 380 degrees.
2. Place the frozen egg rolls in the air fryer not touching and cook them for 8 to 10 minutes.
3. Remove them from the air fryer, let cool slightly, then enjoy!*
4. *reheat at 350 degrees for 3 minutes, preheated

Notes

HOW TO COOK FROZEN SPRING ROLLS IN THE AIR FRYER

Preheat your air fryer to 400 degrees.

Place frozen spring rolls in the air fryer and cook for 7 to 8 minutes until warmed thoroughly. Remove from the air fryer and enjoy!

reheat at 350 degrees for 2 to 3 minutes, preheated

HOW TO COOK FROZEN MINI EGG ROLLS IN THE AIR FRYER

Preheat your air fryer to 380 degrees.

Place the frozen mini egg rolls in the air fryer and cook for 5 to 7 minutes until warmed thoroughly. Remove them from the air fryer and enjoy!*

reheat at 350 degrees for about 2 minutes

Air Fryer Cinnamon Roll Bites

Servings: 4

Cooking Time: 6 Minutes

Ingredients:

- 1 can cinnamon rolls I use Pillsbury

Directions:

1. Open the canned cinnamon rolls, remove the icing to a small bowl, and set it aside.
2. Use a knife to cut the cinnamon rolls into equal pieces. Take each piece of cinnamon roll and hand roll it until they are small round dough balls.
3. Place the cinnamon roll bites in a single layer into the prepared basket of the air fryer.

4. Air fry cinnamon rolls at 320 degrees Fahrenheit for 6 minutes or until golden brown, flipping the bites halfway through.
5. Carefully remove the cinnamon roll bites from the air fryer basket and serve with the icing as a dipping sauce.

Notes

I make this recipe in my Cosori 5.8 qt. air fryer or 6.8 quart air fryer. Depending on your air fryer, size and wattages, cooking time may need to be adjusted 1-2 minutes.

Store remaining bites in an airtight container in the refrigerator for up to 3 days. To reheat, add the cinnamon bites back to the air fryer and reheat at 320 degrees Fahrenheit for 1-2 minutes, or until they are heated through.

Crispy Spinach Tacos

Servings: 9

Cooking Time: 20 Minutes

Ingredients:

- 9 small spinach tortillas (5-inch diameter)
- 2 cups of (360 g) cooked rice
- 1 (15 oz) can kidney beans or black beans (rinsed and drained)
- 1 small/medium onion diced
- ½ tbsp oil
- 2 garlic cloves minced
- ½ bell pepper chopped
- ¾ cup (100 g) canned mushrooms or use fresh
- ½ tsp onion powder
- ½ tsp ground cumin
- ½ tsp paprika
- ¼ tsp smoked paprika
- ¼ tsp ground ginger (optional)
- ¼ tsp black pepper or more to taste
- sea salt to taste
- 1 tbsp balsamic vinegar
- 1 tbsp soy sauce (gluten-free if needed)
- 4 tbsp plant-based milk
- ⅓ cup (80 g) passata

- 2 tbsp hot sauce (or use less/more to taste)
- 1 batch (200 g) vegan cheese sauce or use 7 oz store-bought vegan cheese

Directions:

1. Cook rice according to package instructions. You will need 2 cups of cooked rice for this recipe.
2. Prepare the spinach tortillas (click for the recipe) or use store-bought flour tortillas or corn tortillas of choice.
3. Meanwhile, heat oil in a pan/skillet over medium heat and add the onion, mushrooms, and bell pepper.
4. Sauté for about 3-5 minutes, then add garlic for a further minute. Stir occasionally.
5. Add all spices, balsamic vinegar, soy sauce, plant-based milk, passata, and hot sauce. Stir and let simmer for about 3 minutes.
6. Add cooked rice and beans, stir and turn off the heat.
7. Taste and adjust seasoning if needed.
8. Preheat oven to 410 degrees Fahrenheit (210 degrees Celsius) and line a baking sheet with parchment paper.
9. Make one batch of the vegan cheese sauce or use store-bought vegan cheese.
10. Add about 2 tbsp of the rice filling on one side of a tortilla and 1 tbsp of the vegan cheese. Fold the other side over the filling and press it slightly down with your fingers (see pictures above in the blog post). Do the same for the remaining tortillas.
11. Transfer all tortillas to the baking sheet. Bake in the oven for about 10-15 minutes, or until crispy. Enjoy hot!
12. Check the blog post for the air-fryer method.

Air Fryer French Toast

Ingredients:

- 4 slices brioche bread
- 2 eggs
- 1/4 cup cream
- 1 tsp vanilla essence
- Cinnamon and sugar
- 80g milk chocolate
- 80ml cream

Directions:

1. Cut bread slices in three fingers, and coat in mixture made from whisked eggs, cream and vanilla. Dip one side of your slice (all around coating and it's too sweet, for me) in cinnamon and sugar before placing in the air fryer, sugared side up. Bake at 200°C for 5 minutes, and turn halfway. No need to wait for the air fryer to heat up - place in as soon as you've put it on. Enjoy with chocolate ganache, heat your cream and throw in your chopped chocolate. Let it sit for a few minutes to melt, then mix through. Enjoy!

Air Fryer Blueberry Baked Oats

Servings: 4
Cooking Time: 10-30 Minutes

Ingredients:

- 2 free-range eggs
- 400ml/14fl oz milk
- 4 tbsp runny honey or maple syrup
- 200g/7oz porridge oats
- 2 tsp baking powder
- large pinch salt
- 100g/3½oz fresh blueberries or any frozen berries
- plain yoghurt, to serve (optional)

Directions:

1. Beat together the eggs, milk and honey in a large bowl. Add the oats, baking powder and salt to the bowl, stirring until well mixed. If you have time, leave to sit for 5–10 minutes so the oats can soak up the milk. Preheat the air fryer to 175C.

2. Divide the mixture between four small heatproof dishes or 150ml/5fl oz ramekins and then scatter over the blueberries.

3. Air fry for 10–12 minutes until golden and set. Serve warm or chilled, topped with a spoonful of yoghurt, if using.

4. Recipe Tips

5. Make the mixture the night before and store covered in the fridge to make breakfast even faster in the morning. Remove from the fridge to allow to come to room temperature before topping with blueberries and cooking.

6. If you don't have an air fryer you can bake these in an oven preheated to 200C/180C Fan/Gas 6 for 20-25 minutes.

Air Fryer Banana Nut Bread

Servings: 6

Cooking Time: 25 Minutes

Ingredients:

- 1 1/2 cups all purpose flour
- 1 teaspoon baking powder
- 1/2 cup sugar
- 1/3 cup brown sugar
- 1/3 cup unsalted butter melted
- 1 large egg
- 1/2 teaspoon vanilla extract
- 2 medium bananas overripe
- 1/3 cup walnuts chopped

Directions:

1. In a medium bowl, stir together the flour and baking powder. Set bowl aside.

2. In a large mixing bowl, beat together the butter, sugar, and brown sugar. Add in the egg and vanilla. Continue mixing until well combined.

3. Stir in the flour mixture and mix together until it forms into a slightly wet dough.

4. Add mashed bananas to the batter, and mix on slow speed, or using a wooden spoon, until they are thoroughly mixed into the batter. Add in the chopped nuts, and stir until evenly distributed throughout the batter.

5. Pour the mixture into a lightly sprayed or lined cake pan, or smaller loaf pans, filling ⅔ full. Place the pan or pans into the air fryer basket.

6. Cook at 310 degrees Fahrenheit for 23-25 minutes. Once you remove the dough from the loaf pan, if they are still moist on the bottom of the loaf, return to the air fryer and cook an additional minute or two until the bottom is cooked.

Notes

This recipe makes 2-3 mini loaves, 1- seven inch round loaf, and 1 traditional size loaf of bread. If using a large loaf pan, the cooking time will need to be adjusted. The smaller pans allow the bread to cook much faster.

If bananas aren't well mashed, and incorporated into the batter well, the center may not cook properly.

Air Fryer French Toast Sticks

Servings: 4

Cooking Time: 10 Minutes

Ingredients:

- 5 slices of bread
- 2 eggs
- 1/3 cup milk
- 3 tablespoons sugar
- 2 tablespoons flour
- 1 teaspoon ground cinnamon
- 1/2 teaspoon vanilla extract
- 1/8 teaspoon salt
- OPTIONAL
- Confectioners sugar for dusting
- Maple syrup for dipping

Directions:

1. Preheat your air fryer to 370 degrees.

2. Cut each piece of bread into 3 equal pieces and set aside.

3. Put the eggs, milk, flour, sugar, vanilla, ground cinnamon, and salt into a wide shallow dish. Whisk to combine.

4. Dip each piece of bread into the egg mixture, making sure to coat on all sides.

5. Place a piece of parchment round paper inside the air fryer and place each french toast stick in one

single layer on top of the parchment round (needed to prevent sticking).

6. Cook for about 10 minutes, flipping halfway through.

7. Carefully remove the air fryer french toast sticks from the air fryer and enjoy immediately, store in the fridge for up to 3 days, or freeze up to 3 months.

Notes

HOW TO REHEAT FRENCH TOAST STICKS IN THE AIR FRYER:

Preheat your air fryer to 350 degrees.

Cook french toast sticks for 2-3 minutes until warmed and enjoy!

HOW TO COOK FROZEN FRENCH TOAST STICKS IN THE AIR FRYER:

Preheat your air fryer to 320 degrees.

Cook frozen french toast sticks in the air fryer for 2-3 minutes until warmed and enjoy!

Air Fryer Ham And Swiss Crescent Rolls

Servings: 4

Ingredients:

- 1 can (8 oz) refrigerated Pillsbury™ Original Crescent Rolls (8 Count)
- 8 thin slices deli ham (3.5 oz)
- 4 thin slices Swiss cheese (3 oz), each cut into 4 strips

Directions:

1. Cut 8-inch round of cooking parchment paper; place in bottom of air fryer basket.

2. Unroll dough; separate into 8 triangles. Place 1 piece of ham on each triangle; place 2 strips of cheese down center of ham. Fold in edges of ham to match shape of dough triangle. Roll up each crescent, ending at tip of triangle.

3. On parchment paper in air fryer basket, place 4 crescent rolls point sides down. Cover remaining crescent rolls with plastic wrap, and refrigerate.

4. Set air fryer to 300°F; cook 6 minutes. With tongs, turn over each one; cook 4 to 7 minutes longer or

until golden brown. Remove from air fryer. Repeat with remaining 4 crescent rolls. Serve warm.

Cheese & Veggie Egg Cups

Ingredients:

- 4 eggs, large
- 1 cup veggies of your choice, diced
- 1 cup shredded cheese
- 4 tbsp half and half
- 1 tbsp cilantro, chopped
- salt and pepper, for sprinkling
- cooking spray

Directions:

1. Grease your air fryer safe muffin tin and set aside.

2. In a medium mixing bowl, whisk together the eggs, vegetables, half the cheese, half and half, cilantro, salt and pepper together.

3. Divide the mixture evenly into each cup of the muffin tin and place it in the air fryer. Air fry at 300°F for 12 minutes. Then, top the cups with the remaining cheese and air fry at 400°F for another 1-2 minutes, or until lightly browned.

4. Serve immediately and enjoy!

Air Fryer Cauliflower Tacos

Servings: 4

Ingredients:

- FOR THE SLAW
- 1 c. thinly sliced red cabbage
- 1/2 small red onion, diced
- 1 jalapeño, minced
- 1 clove garlic, minced
- Juice of 1 lime
- 2 tbsp. apple cider vinegar
- Pinch kosher salt
- FOR THE CAULIFLOWER
- 1 1/2 c. all-purpose flour
- 1 tsp. chili powder
- 1 tsp. cumin
- 1/2 tsp. garlic powder
- 1/2 tsp. cayenne pepper

- Kosher salt
- Freshly ground black pepper
- 1 1/2 c. almond milk or other non-dairy milk
- 1 1/2 c. panko bread crumbs
- 1 medium head cauliflower, cut into bite-size florets
- Cooking spray
- FOR SERVING
- 1/2 c. vegan mayonnaise
- 2 tbsp. sriracha
- 1 tsp. maple syrup
- Corn tortillas
- Sliced avocado
- Freshly chopped cilantro
- Lime wedges

Directions:

1. In a medium bowl, combine slaw ingredients. Let sit while prepping tacos, stirring every so often.
2. In a medium bowl, combine flour and spices and season well with salt and pepper. Add almond milk and stir to combine. Mixture should be thick, but still easy to dip cauliflower into. Add a little more milk if needed. Place panko into small bowl.
3. Dip florets into milk mixture, wiping any excess off, then toss in panko.
4. Working in batches, place coated cauliflower into basket of air fryer and spray with cooking spray. Cook at 400° for 15 minutes, stopping about halfway through to toss and spray with more cooking spray.
5. In a small bowl, combine vegan mayonnaise, sriracha, and maple syrup.
6. Assemble tacos: On a tortilla top with cooked cauliflower, avocado, pickled slaw, cilantro, and a drizzle of sriracha mayo. Serve with lime wedges.

Air Fryer Breakfast Potatoes

Servings: 4
Cooking Time: 15 Minutes

Ingredients:

- 1 pound russet potatoes, peeled and cut into ½" cubes
- 1 red pepper, chopped into 1" pieces
- 1 small onion, roughly chopped
- 2 tablespoons oil
- ½ teaspoon salt
- Fresh parsley for garnish

Directions:

1. Preheat your air fryer to 390 F.
2. Toss the potatoes, pepper, and onion with the oil, and salt.
3. Transfer to the air fryer basket, then cook for 15 minutes, tossing halfway through.
4. Garnish with fresh parsley and serve immediately with eggs.

Notes

HOW TO REHEAT BREAKFAST POTATOES:
Preheat your air fryer to 390 degrees.
Add potatoes to the air fryer basket and cook for 3-4 minutes or until hot and crispy.

Air Fryer Pizza Egg Rolls

Servings: 4
Cooking Time: 10 Minutes

Ingredients:

- 8 egg roll wrappers
- 8 mozzarella cheese sticks
- pepperoni slices
- ¼ cup pizza sauce

Directions:

1. Lay out wrappers with corners left and right. Add a small spoonful of pizza sauce onto the center of the eggroll wrapper.
2. Add 3-4 slices of pepperonis, overlapping pieces, then top with a mozzarella cheese stick. Fold bottom corn over the filling and tuck under.

3. Next, fold in the left and right corners, and then turn over, to make a large pillow shape.
4. Lightly spray the air fryer basket, and place each Egg Roll in the basket without stacking or overlapping. Lightly spray each egg roll to help with crispness and color.
5. Air fry at 400 degrees F for 10-12 minutes, until golden and crispy. Turn halfway during the air frying process.
6. Serve with marinara or pizza sauce for dipping. Garnish with parsley flakes.

Notes

Variations

Add different ingredients - Don't forget that you can easily add your favorite pizza toppings to the middle of these golden brown egg rolls. You can make cheese pizza egg rolls only, or add extra pizza sauce, turkey pepperoni, diced green pepper, black olives, or any other different flavors that you want to add.

Air Fryer Falafel

Servings: 25
Cooking Time: 15 Minutes

Ingredients:

- 2 cups (400 g) dried chickpeas (not canned or cooked chickpeas)
- 5 garlic cloves chopped
- 1 small onion chopped
- 1 cup parsley leaves chopped
- 1/2 cup cilantro leaves chopped
- 2 tsp ground coriander
- 2 tsp ground cumin
- 1 1/2 tsp sea salt
- 1 tsp black pepper
- Red pepper flakes or cayenne pepper to taste
- 1 tsp baking powder (optional, see notes)
- Cooking spray

Directions:

1. Watch the video in the post for easy visual instructions.

2. The day before you start making the falafel, place the dried chickpeas in a large bowl. Fill it with plenty of water (the chickpeas should be covered by at least 3 inches/7 cm but add more water if needed) and soak for 18-24 hours. Drain the chickpeas completely and use a paper towel to lightly pat dry them (if they are too wet).
3. Transfer the chickpeas along with all other ingredients to a large food processor. If you have a small food processor, you will need to work in batches. Process everything for about 20 seconds, then scrape down the sides of the food processor and blend again. Do this a few times until the mixture is well combined, but not mushy.
4. Refrigerate the falafel mixture (in the food processor bowl) for about 45-60 minutes (or longer).
5. Use an ice cream scooper to scoop the falafel mixture and shape it with your hands to form a ball (or make a patty/disk if you wish). Do this with the remaining falafel mixture.
6. Use the cooking spray to lightly spray the falafel balls. Also, spray the basket of your air fryer to avoid sticking. Heat the air fryer to 375 °F (190 °C) and set the timer to 15 minutes. Cook the falafel balls in the air fryer, flip them after 10 minutes. They should be crispy and slightly brown on the outside. You might need to fry them in batches if necessary.
7. Serve hot on its own or assemble the falafels in pita bread with tahini, lettuce, tomato, and cucumbers. Enjoy!

Notes

Make sure to use dried chickpeas, not canned or cooked chickpeas.

Flour: I didn't add any flour to the falafel mixture because it held very well together and didn't require a binder. However, if you notice that your mixture needs a binder, you can add 2 tablespoons of chickpea flour (or regular flour or cornstarch). Especially, if you plan to deep-fry them, then adding flour is highly recommended!

Baking powder: You can optionally add a little baking powder to the falafel mix, and it'll result in slightly lighter and airier, tender falafel. Add it just before frying (i.e. don't add it to the mixture when making ahead and chilling in the fridge or freezing).

Oven-baked falafel: It's better to shape the falafel mixture into patties if you want to oven-bake them. Bake in a 375ºF (190ºC) heated oven for about 25-30 minutes, flipping halfway through. I also recommend spraying them with oil (cooking spray) before baking and after flipping, as they will turn out crispier.

If you want to deep-fry them, fill a large frying pan or medium saucepan with oil (to a depth of about 2 1/2 or 3 inches) and heat it to about 360 ºF (180 ºC). Make sure the oil isn't too hot, or they might fall apart. Add in a couple of falafel balls/patties (don't overcrowd the pan) and fry for about 4 minutes, turning as needed. Place the fried falafel on paper towels to soak up excess oil. It is important that the mixture rested in the refrigerator for about 60 minutes before frying. Also, if you think they are still too moist, then roll the balls/patties in some flour.

You can freeze the uncooked falafel balls for up to a month.

Check the helpful tips and step-by-step photos in the blog post above.

The total time doesn't include the soaking- and resting time.

Air Fryer Eggplant Parmesan

Servings: 4
Cooking Time: 20 Minutes

Ingredients:

- ½ cup Italian bread crumbs
- ¼ cup freshly grated Parmesan cheese
- 1 teaspoon Italian seasoning
- 1 teaspoon salt
- ½ teaspoon dried basil
- ½ teaspoon garlic powder
- ½ teaspoon onion powder
- ½ teaspoon freshly ground black pepper
- ¼ cup flour

- 2 large eggs, beaten
- 1 medium eggplant, sliced into 1/2-inch rounds
- 1 cup marinara sauce, or more to taste
- 8 slices mozzarella cheese, or as needed

Directions:

1. Combine bread crumbs, Parmesan cheese, Italian seasoning, salt, basil, garlic powder, onion powder, and black pepper in a shallow bowl. Place flour in a separate shallow bowl and beaten eggs in a third shallow bowl.
2. Dip sliced eggplant first in flour, then in beaten eggs, and finally coat with bread crumb mixture. Place coated eggplant on a tray and let rest for 5 minutes.
3. Preheat an air fryer to 370 degrees F (185 degrees C).
4. Place breaded eggplant rounds in the air fryer basket, making sure they are not touching; work in batches if necessary. Cook for 8 to 10 minutes, flip each round, and cook until desired crispiness is achieved, 4 to 6 minutes more.
5. Top each eggplant round with marinara sauce and 1 slice of mozzarella cheese. Place the basket back in the air fryer and cook until cheese has started to melt, 1 to 2 minutes. Repeat with remaining eggplant, if necessary.
6. Serve hot and enjoy!

Easy Air Fryer Pizza Roll Ups

Servings: 4
Cooking Time: 5 Minutes

Ingredients:

- 4 8 inch flour tortillas
- 4 tablespoons pizza sauce
- 20 slices pepperoni
- 2 mozzarella string cheese
- 1 teaspoon olive oil

Directions:

1. Warm the tortillas: Stack the 4 tortillas onto a microwavable safe plate and place a damp paper towel on top. Microwave for 20 seconds until the

tortillas are warm. You can also use a tortilla warmer if you have one.

2. Preheat the air fryer to 375 degrees Fahrenheit and set the time for 5 minutes.

3. Cut the string cheese in half lengthwise.

4. Lay a tortilla flat and add about 1 tablespoon of pizza sauce at the bottom. Add 5 pepperoni slices on top of the pizza sauce, then add the string cheese on top of the pepperoni and roll all of the ingredients into a roll up. Repeat for each tortilla until you have 4 roll ups.

5. Brush the top of each roll up evenly with olive oil as this will add a little extra crispiness to the roll ups.

6. Add the pizza roll ups to the air fryer, seam down, add cook for 5 minutes or until the pizza roll ups are golden brown.

7. Carefully remove the pizza rolls ups from the air fryer, let cool, then enjoy! These taste great dipped in some pizza sauce.

Notes

Warm up your tortillas before rolling them. This will make them easier to roll without cracking.

Go easy on the pizza sauce. When assembling the pizza rolls, be sure to use no more than a tablespoon of pizza sauce on each roll up. If you use too much sauce it will just spill out of the tortilla.

Be sure to let the pizza roll ups cool down before eating as they will be very hot when they first come out of the air fryer.

Every air fryer is different so be sure to check for doneness halfway through. The air fryer I used to test this recipe was my Instant Vortex Plus 6 quart.

Store leftovers in the refrigerator in an airtight container for up to 4 days.

To reheat, preheat the air fryer to 360 degrees Fahrenheit and heat pizza roll ups for 1-2 minutes.

Air Fryer Soft Boiled Eggs

Servings: 4
Cooking Time: 6 Minutes

Ingredients:

- 4 large eggs

Directions:

1. Place the eggs in a small ramekin or silicone dish, or in the air fryer basket.

2. Air fry at 300 degrees F for 6-8 minutes. (Six minutes for very runny yolks and whites, 8 minutes for more firm whites, but still slightly runny yolks)

3. When done air frying, place eggs into an ice bath until they are warm to the touch. Gently peel eggs and serve as desired.

4. If using eggs as "dippy eggs," place slightly cooled eggs in egg holders, and gently crack tops with a spoon, and remove the top shells.

Air Fryer Nutella French Toast Roll-ups

Servings: 4
Cooking Time: 6 Minutes

Ingredients:

- 10 slices of bread
- 3 large eggs
- 2 tbsp milk
- 4 tbsp granulated white sugar
- 1 tsp cinnamon
- 10 tsp Nutella

Directions:

1. If you haven't already, lay the bread out for 30 minutes to an hour to allow it to become stale.

2. If you're planning ahead, you can leave the bread out over night.

3. Whisk together the eggs and milk and set aside.

4. In a small dish, mix the cinnamon and sugar and set aside.

5. Cut the crust off of the slices of bread and then take a glass or rolling pin to flatten the bread.

6. Take a teaspoon of Nutella and spread on one end of the flattened bread. Roll the bread up, and dab a

little Nutella on the end to help keep the rolls closed and secure during cooking.

7. Dip the french toast roll-ups in the egg mixture and then roll into the cinnamon and sugar mixture.

8. Place the Nutella French Toast Rolls ups into the prepared air fryer basket. Cook on 360 degrees Fahrenheit for 5-6 minutes, flipping the roll-ups halfway through.

9. Serve immediately.

Notes

You can use just about anything if you don't have Nutella. Strawberries, blueberries, apples, peanut butter and jelly, or just skip the filling and leave them plain. Either way, they are delicious!

Air Fryer German Pancake Bites

Ingredients:

- Pancakes:
- 6 eggs
- 1 cup whole milk
- 1 tsp salt
- 1 cup all-purpose flour
- Toppings Options:
- Chocolate hazelnut spread
- Berries
- Banana slices

Directions:

1. In a large bowl, beat together eggs and milk. Sift in flour and salt. MIx well with electric mixer and set aside.

2. Lightly butter ramekins or 4 small oven-safe cups. Fill each container 1/4 full of batter.

3. Place in air fryer and set to 400F for 6 minutes.

4. Carefully remove pancake bites from ramekins and top with your favorite toppings!

5. Enjoy!

SALADS & SIDE DISHES RECIPES

Cardamom Roasted Beetroot Salad With Harissa Tahini Sauce

Servings: 4

Ingredients:

- For the roasted beets
- 500g beetroot (peeled, chopped into 2cm pieces)
- 1 x 400g organic chickpeas (drained, rinsed, patted dry)
- 1 1/2 tbsp olive oil
- 1 tbsp agave nectar
- 2 tsp ground cumin
- 16 Seeds from green cardamom pods (ground in pestle and mortar)
- 1 1/4 tsp sea salt
- 1/2 tsp garlic powder
- 1/4 tsp ground black pepper
- 1 Zest of lemon
- For the sauce
- 80g light tahini
- 190ml lukewarm water
- 1 tbsp rose harissa
- 2 tsp agave nectar
- 1 clove garlic (peeled)
- 1 tsp red wine vinegar
- 1/4 tsp ground cumin
- 1/4 - 1/2 tsp sea salt
- 1/2 - 1 Juice of whole lemon
- For the salad
- 100g pomegranate seeds (roughly 1/2 pomegranate)
- 60g rocket
- 30g walnuts (roughly chopped)
- 20g fresh parsley (roughly chopped)
- 1/2 tsp za'atar
- COOKING MODE
- When entering cooking mode - We will enable your screen to stay 'always on' to avoid any unnecessary interruptions whilst you cook!

Directions:

1. Toss together all of the ingredients for the roasted beets in a large bowl until everything is fully coated.
2. Place the crisper tray into the zone 1 drawer then add the vegetables and insert the drawer back into the unit. Select ROAST, set the temperature to 180°C and the temperature to 25 minutes. Select START/STOP to begin cooking. Shake the drawer every 10 minutes until the cooking time is complete. Remove the drawer and set to one side.
3. Place the ingredients for the sauce into a bullet style blender and blend until smooth. Start with the juice of half a lemon and add more if you feel it needs it. Again if you'd prefer a thinner sauce blend in more water.
4. Toss together the roasted beetroot mixture in a large salad bowl with the remaining salad ingredients then serve immediately with plenty of the sauce drizzled over.

Air Fryer Roasted Butternut Squash Salad

Servings: 4
Cooking Time: 15 Minutes

Ingredients:

- 1 small butternut squash, peeled, seeded, cut into 1-inch pieces
- 4 tablespoons olive oil
- 1 teaspoon 's House Seasoning
- 1/4 teaspoon cayenne pepper
- 2 tablespoons fresh lemon juice
- 1 small shallot, minced
- 1/4 teaspoon salt
- 6 ounces arugula
- 1 small Granny Smith apple, cored and thinly sliced
- 1/2 cup toasted sliced almonds
- 1/2 cup grated Parmesan cheese

Directions:

1. In a large bowl, combine squash, 2 tablespoons of the olive oil, House Seasoning, and cayenne pepper; toss to coat well.
2. Place squash in air fryer basket, set air fryer temperature to 400 degrees, and cook for 15 minutes, shaking occasionally. Let cool.
3. In a large bowl, whisk together lemon juice, shallot, salt, and remaining olive oil. Add arugula and toss to coat. Divide arugula between 4 salad plates and top with squash and apple slices. Sprinkle with sliced almonds and Parmesan cheese. Serve chilled.

Air Fryer Pigs In A Blanket

Servings: 10
Cooking Time: 8 Minutes

Ingredients:

- 1 can crescent rolls
- 24 cocktail sausages

Directions:

1. Preheat the air fryer to 350 degrees Fahrenheit. Prepare the air fryer basket with nonstick cooking spray, or once the air fryer has been preheated, add parchment paper.
2. Take a pizza cutter and slice each crescent dough sheet into thirds.
3. Take the cut crescent dough and wrap the dough around the sausage.
4. Place the crescent dogs into the prepared air fryer basket in a single layer and make sure to allow an inch or two between each crescent sausage. You may need to cook in batches if needed.
5. Air fry on 350 degrees Fahrenheit for 3-4 minutes, flip, and then air fry for an additional 3-4 minutes, or until the crescents are golden brown.
6. Carefully remove from the air fryer basket and serve with your favorite dipping sauces.

Notes

This recipe was made using the Cosori 5.8 qt air fryer. If you are using a different air fryer, your cook time may need to be adjusted up or down depending on the wattage and power of the heating element.

WHAT DIPPING SAUCES CAN I USE FOR PIGS IN A BLANKET?
I love to use ketchup and mustard, but you can also use bbq sauce, cheese sauce, honey mustard sauce, ranch dressing, and more.
CAN I COOK FROZEN PIGS IN A BLANKET IN THE AIR FRYER?
Absolutely! If you are cooking these pigs in a blanket from frozen, you will want to add a minute or two to the cooking time to ensure they are cooked completely.

Air Fryer Asparagus Salad With Feta Vinaigrette

Servings: 4

Ingredients:

- 1 lb. asparagus
- 2 tbsp. olive oil, divided
- Kosher salt and pepper
- 1 tbsp. rice vinegar
- 1 small shallot, finely chopped
- 1/4 c. fresh mint, finely chopped
- 2 oz. feta, crumbled
- 2 tbsp. fresh dill, roughly chopped

Directions:

1. Heat oven to 425°F. On a small rimmed baking sheet, toss asparagus with 1 tablespoon oil and ¼ teaspoon each salt and pepper. Roast until just tender, 8 to 12 minutes; transfer to platter.
2. Meanwhile, in small bowl, combine vinegar, shallot and ¼ teaspoon each salt and pepper. Let sit, tossing occasionally, until asparagus is done.
3. Stir remaining tablespoon oil into shallot mixture, then gently toss with mint and feta. Spoon over asparagus and sprinkle with dill.
4. AIR FRYING INSTRUCTIONS:
5. Heat air fryer to 400°F. Toss asparagus with 1 tablespoon olive oil and 1/4 teaspoon each salt and pepper. Air-fry, shaking basket halfway through, until tender, 10 minutes. Proceed with steps 2-3.

Crispy Parmesan Potato Wedges

Servings: 2

Ingredients:

- 2 small russet potatoes
- 2 tablespoons (28 grams) Parmesan cheese, grated
- ¾ teaspoon (4 grams) salt
- ¼ teaspoon (2 grams) garlic powder
- ¼ teaspoon (2 grams) paprika
- ¼ teaspoon (2 grams) dried oregano
- 1 tablespoon (15 milliliters) neutral-flavored oil

Directions:

1. Cut each potato lengthwise into 8 wedges and place them in a large bowl.
2. Add the remaining ingredients and toss to coat.
3. Place the crisper plate into the Smart Air Fryer basket, then place the potatoes onto the crisper plate.
4. Select the Fries function, adjust time to 22 minutes, and press Start/Pause.
5. Remove the potato wedges when done and serve.

Air Fryer Roasted Garlic

Servings: 1/2

Cooking Time: 10 Minutes

Ingredients:

- 3 full bulbs garlic
- 1-2 tablespoons olive oil
- 1 teaspoon salt

Directions:

1. Preheat air fryer to 400 F
2. Carefully slice the tops off the garlic bulbs; the cloves inside should be exposed.
3. Drizzle the olive oil over top of each garlic bulb, making sure all the cloves get covered.
4. Sprinkle salt on each bulb and tightly wrap each in tin foil.
5. Place garlic into your air fryer and cook for 18-20 minutes, or until garlic is tender.
6. Allow to cool until you can handle and remove the bulbs from the papery skin.

Air Fryer Garlic Knots

Servings: 6

Cooking Time: 8 Minutes

Ingredients:

- 1 can store-bought pizza dough 13.8 ounces or two cans of thin crust pizza 8 ounces each
- 4 tablespoons unsalted butter melted
- 1/4 cup parmesan cheese grated
- 2 cloves garlic minced
- 1 tablespoon dried parsley flakes
- 1 teaspoon Italian Seasoning

Directions:

1. Open the can of premade pizza dough and on a lightly floured surface, roll it out into a rectangle.
2. With a pizza cutter or kitchen knife cut the dough into twelve 1-inch strips, and then fold each strip in half. Tie each piece into dough knots, making 12 knots.
3. Place the dough balls into the air fryer basket in a single layer, lined with parchment paper, a silicone baking mat or lightly sprayed with olive oil spray.
4. Air fry at 350 degrees F for 8-10 minutes, until they are golden brown.
5. While knots are in a small mixing bowl, stir together the melted butter, parmesan cheese, garlic, parsley flakes, and Italian seasoning.
6. When knots are golden brown, use a pastry brush and generously brush garlic butter on each piece with butter and seasonings and top with grated parmesan cheese.

Notes

Kitchen Tips: Make these in batches without overcrowding the basket. Use a food scale to ensure they are all the same size, so they cook evenly. To get a deeper brown color cook for 1 additional minute.

If using regular crust dough, knots will be just a tad bit thicker and may need 1-2 additional minutes of air frying time.

For smaller bites, just cut the dough in half, and you will have 24 garlic knots.

Optional Favorite Dipping Sauce: Our favorite sauce for dipping is marinara. But you can use other sauces, like homemade marinara sauce, alfredo sauce, pesto sauce, pizza sauce or Greek yogurt with roasted garlic.

Artichoke Wings With Vegan Ranch Dip

Servings: 6

Ingredients:

- Artichoke Wings
- One 16-ounce jar marinated artichoke hearts
- 1½ cups all-purpose flour
- 1 teaspoon garlic powder
- 1 teaspoon onion powder
- 1 teaspoon paprika
- 1 teaspoon kosher salt
- One 12-ounce bottle beer (Lager or Weisse-style for best results)
- 2 cups panko breadcrumbs
- Vegan Ranch Dip
- 1 cup vegan mayonnaise
- ¼ cup non-dairy milk (i.e., coconut, oat, or any nut milk)
- 2 tablespoons fresh dill, finely chopped
- 1 teaspoon fresh Italian parsley leaves, finely chopped
- 1 teaspoon vegan Worcestershire sauce (optional)
- 1 teaspoon apple cider vinegar
- 1 teaspoon lemon juice
- 1 clove garlic, grated
- 1 teaspoon onion powder
- 1 teaspoon black pepper
- Kosher salt, to taste
- Oil spray

Directions:

1. Select the Preheat function on the Air Fryer then press Start/Pause.
2. Drain the artichoke hearts and pat dry with paper towels.
3. Whisk together the flour, garlic powder, onion powder, paprika, and salt in a large bowl until evenly distributed.
4. Pour in the beer and whisk well until no lumps remain. The mixture should resemble pancake batter.
5. Place the panko breadcrumbs in a separate medium bowl.
6. Line the preheated air fryer baskets with parchment paper.
7. Dredge the artichoke hearts in the beer batter, then roll in the panko breadcrumbs.
8. Shake off any excess breadcrumbs, then place the dredged artichoke hearts into the lined air fryer baskets.
9. Spray the wings lightly with oil and insert into the preheated air fryer.
10. Adjust temperature to 400°F and time to 10 minutes, press Shake, then press Start/Pause.
11. Flip the wings and spray again halfway through cooking. The Shake Reminder will let you know when.
12. Combine all the dressing ingredients in a separate medium bowl and whisk together.
13. Season to taste with kosher salt. Pour into a bowl for dipping.
14. Remove the artichoke wings from the air fryer when done.
15. Serve immediately with the vegan ranch dressing.

Air Fryer Sweet Potato Casserole

Servings: 6
Cooking Time: 10 Minutes

Ingredients:

- 29 ounce sweet potato yams drained
- 3/4 cup pecans
- 1/4 teaspoon salt
- 1 egg
- 1/2 teaspoon vanilla extract
- 1/4 teaspoon ground cinnamon
- 1 1/4 cup granulated white sugar
- 1 Tablespoon heavy cream

- 2 Tablespoons unsalted butter softened

Directions:

1. Preheat the air fryer to 350 degrees Fahrenheit.
2. Place the sweet potatoes into a medium sized mixing bowl. Add the salt, butter, egg, vanilla extract, ground cinnamon, white sugar, and heavy cream. Mix thoroughly for one minute.
3. Place the pecans in a food processor. Chop the pecans until they are small and easy to sprinkle.
4. Take the sweet potato mixture and place in a prepared 7" springform pan. Cover the top with the chopped pecans.
5. Place the springform pan into the air fryer basket. Air fry for 10-12 minutes or until the topping is browned.

Notes

Can I make a sweet potato casserole in the air fryer with a marshmallow topping?

Yes, you can, but you may want to consider doing it a little differently than the traditional method of topping the casserole with mini marshmallows. Because marshmallows are light and fluffy, they can easily blow around and possibly blow up into the heating element.If you want to have a marshmallow topping, consider using the jarred marshmallow fluff, or push the marshmallows into the casserole so that they don't fly around while air frying.

How do I store leftover sweet potato casserole?

Store leftover sweet potato casserole in an airtight container in the refrigerator for up to 4 days.

How do I reheat leftover air fryer sweet potato casserole?

To reheat leftover casserole, add it to an oven-safe dish and reheat in the air fryer at 350 degrees Fahrenheit for 2-3 minutes, or until the casserole is heated through.

What are additions I can make to sweet potato casserole?

You can change the flavors in sweet potato casserole by adding different ingredients such as diced pineapple. It gives the casserole an even more pronounced flavor and it is delicious!

Air Fryer Diced Potatoes

Servings: 4
Cooking Time: 20 Minutes

Ingredients:

- 1 ½ pounds of small potatoes
- 2 cups cold water
- 1 tablespoon fresh thyme or 1 teaspoon dried thyme
- ½ tablespoon minced garlic
- ½ tablespoon olive oil
- Juice of 1/2 a lemon, about 2 tablespoons of a medium size lemon
- Salt to taste

Directions:

1. Wash your potatoes and dice them into small cubes. The closer they are in size, the more evenly they will cook.
2. Soak the cut potatoes for 10 minutes in cold water. This will help remove some starch and allow them to crisp up more. Once they have soaked, drain them and then pat them dry with a paper towel.
3. Combine potatoes with the thyme, garlic, olive oil and lemon juice.
4. Place diced potatoes in your air fryer basket. Cook at 380 degrees F for 20 to 25 minutes, giving the basket a good shake at the 10 minute mark.

Notes

OPTIONAL

Sprinkle more fresh thyme to the potatoes before serving or some zest from your lemon, or both!

HOW TO REHEAT DICED POTATOES IN THE AIR FRYER

Preheat the air fryer to 350 degrees F.

Lay the leftover diced potatoes in the air fryer basket in a single layer.

Cook for 3 to 5 minutes until heated through.

Air Fryer Kielbasa

Servings: 4

Cooking Time: 8 Minutes

Ingredients:

- 1 package Kielbasa 15 ounces

Directions:

1. To make this kielbasa dish, remove sausage from packaging, and then cut into bite-size pieces (about ½ inch sized coin size pieces.)

2. Transfer to the air fryer basket, and air fry at 380 degrees F for 8-10 minutes. I tossed the pieces of sausage halfway through air frying.

3. Remove from basket and serve!

Notes

How to Air Fry Frozen Kielbasa

If you want to make this from frozen, place it in the air fryer basket, and air fry at 380 degrees F, for 10-12 minutes cooking time.

VEGETABLE & & VEGETARIAN RECIPES

Air Fryer Roasted Rainbow Carrots

Servings: 4
Cooking Time: 6 Minutes

Ingredients:

- ½ pound tri-color carrots 1 inch pieces
- 1 tablespoon olive oil
- 1 tablespoon honey
- salt and pepper to taste

Directions:

1. Preheat the air fryer to 400°F.
2. Toss the carrots with the remaining ingredients until fully coated.
3. Place carrots in the air fryer basket and cook for 7-8 minutes and serve.

Air Fryer Roasted Potatoes

Servings: 4
Cooking Time: 20 Minutes

Ingredients:

- 24 oz petite potatoes
- 1 tbsp olive oil
- 1/2 tsp onion powder
- 1/2 tsp garlic powder
- 1/4 tsp smoked paprika
- 1/4 tsp white pepper
- 1/2 tsp ground black pepper

Directions:

1. Take the potatoes and place them in a colander. Rinse well.
2. Use a knife and cut the petite potatoes in half down the center.
3. Add the cut potatoes to a medium sized mixing bowl. Coat with olive oil and seasonings. Stir well to coat.
4. Add the seasoned potatoes to the basket of the prepared air fryer basket.
5. Cook the potatoes at 400 degrees Fahrenheit for 10 minutes.

6. Open the air fryer and shake the basket. Continue to cook for an additional 6-10 minutes.
7. Remove the roasted potatoes from the air fryer and top them with fresh parsley before serving.

Notes

Every air fryer is different so if you have a stronger powered air fryer, you may need to cut the time a little to ensure you don't overcook the potatoes. I personally find that 16-17 minutes for small petite potato halves in my Cosori 5.8 is perfect. However, you may need to add additional time depending on the size of your potatoes and the brand of air fryer you use.

Air Fryer Stuffed Portobello Mushrooms

Servings: 4
Cooking Time: 15 Minutes

Ingredients:

- 1 pound Italian sausage or ground beef
- ¼ onion diced
- 2 garlic cloves minced
- 1 green pepper diced
- 2 cups tomato sauce
- 1 tablespoon olive oil
- 4 portobello mushroom caps
- ⅓ cup mozzarella shredded
- 1 tablespoon parmesan cheese shredded

Directions:

1. In a large saucepan cook the sausage, garlic, onion, and pepper until tender. Add tomato sauce and let simmer for 10 minutes or until thick.
2. Preheat the air fryer to 350°F.
3. Scoop out the gills of the mushrooms and wash with cold water. Dry thoroughly and drizzle with olive oil.
4. Place mushrooms in the air fryer basket and cook cap side up for 5 minutes.
5. Once done flip mushrooms over and evenly fill with the sausage filling.

6. Top with mozzarella and parmesan cheese, cook for 8-10 minutes or until mushroom is cooked and cheese is melted.

Notes

Mushrooms get soggy so clean them with a spritz of water, and dry with a paper towel, or brush with a damp paper towel.

Gills and stems can be used in the sauce for extra flavor. Store leftovers in an airtight container in the refrigerator for up to 3 days. Set the air fryer at 400°F and reheat for 4 minutes.

Crispy Air Fryer Brussels Sprouts

Ingredients:

- 1 lb. brussels sprouts, trimmed and halved lengthwise (approximately 4 cups)
- 1 tablespoon olive oil
- 1/2 tablespoon Italian seasoning
- 1/2 tablespoon garlic powder
- 1/8 teaspoon salt
- 1/4 teaspoon ground black pepper, or to taste

Directions:

1. Combine all ingredients in a large bowl and toss to combine and coat brussels sprouts evenly. Transfer brussels sprouts to air fryer basket.
2. Turn air fryer on to 350 F and cook for 12 minutes, until brussels sprouts are cooked through and golden brown on the edges.

Notes

These instructions work best with a Philips Air Fryer (1.8 lb/2.75 qt). If you have larger or smaller air fryer, you will have to adjust the cook time. Just check in on the brussels sprouts every 5 minutes to make sure that it cooks through and that they don't burn.

Air Fryer Baby Potatoes

Servings: 4
Cooking Time: 20 Minutes

Ingredients:

- 1 pound baby potatoes
- 1 tablespoon olive oil
- 1 clove garlic minced
- ¼ teaspoon rosemary chopped
- ¼ teaspoon salt and pepper each

Directions:

1. Preheat the air fryer to 400°F.
2. Combine the potatoes, oil, garlic, and seasonings and mix until evenly coated.
3. Place in the air fryer and cook for 18-20 minutes, shaking the basket halfway through.
4. Cook until tender and browned.

Notes

Refrigerate leftovers in an airtight container for up to 3 days.

Freeze leftovers in a zippered bag for up to 6 weeks.

Roasted Air Fryer Carrots

Servings: 4
Cooking Time: 20 Minutes

Ingredients:

- Sweet Carrots
- 1 lb carrots washed, peeled, and chopped into 1 inch pieces
- 2 Tablespoon butter melted
- 2 Tablespoon brown sugar
- ¼ teaspoon salt
- Savory Carrots
- 1 lb medium sized carrots washed and peeled
- 2 Tablespoon olive oil
- ½ teaspoon garlic powder
- ½ teaspoon paprika
- 1/4 cup grated parmesan cheese
- Salt and pepper to taste
- Fresh chopped parsley optional

Directions:

1. Sweet Carrots

2. Pour melted butter, brown sugar, salt over carrots and stir until the carrots are fully coated.
3. Place carrots in an oven safe bowl that will fit in your air fryer. Cook on 380 degrees Fahrenheit for 20-25 minutes, stirring halfway.
4. Savory Carrots
5. Place carrots in a large bowl and toss with olive oil, garlic powder, and paprika.
6. Place in the air fryer basket and cook on 380 degrees Fahrenheit for 20 minutes, shaking halfway through. Once done, top with parmesan cheese and parsley. Salt and pepper to taste.

Air Fryer Baked Sweet Potatoes

Servings: 3
Cooking Time: 40 Minutes

Ingredients:
- 3 medium sweet potatoes
- 1 tbsp olive oil
- 1/2 tsp kosher salt
- Toppings (Optional)
- 3 tbsp butter
- 1 1/2 tsp cinnamon
- 1 1/2 tsp brown sugar

Directions:
1. Preheat the air fryer to 390 degrees Fahrenheit and prepare the air fryer basket.
2. Wash and clean the sweet potatoes.
3. Cover the sweet potatoes with the olive oil. Take afork and lightly prick the skin all over for each of the sweet potatoes.
4. Cover the sweet potatoes with kosher salt.
5. Place the sweet potatoes in a single layer in the basket of the air fryer. Cook on 390 degrees Fahrenheit for 40-45 minutes.
6. Carefully remove the sweet potatoes from the air fryer basket.
7. Slice open the sweet cooked potatoes, fluff the sweet potato flesh, and top with butter, cinnamon, and brown sugar. Serve.

Notes

All air fryers cook differently. If you are using small-sized sweet potatoes, consider lowering the time down to 35 minutes and then check to ensure they are done before pulling them. Larger sweet potatoes can take a little longer to cook, consider adding a few minutes to the cook time.

Air-fryer Green Tomato Stacks

Servings: 4
Cooking Time: 15 Minutes

Ingredients:
- 1/4 cup fat-free mayonnaise
- 1/4 teaspoon grated lime zest
- 2 tablespoons lime juice
- 1 teaspoon minced fresh thyme or 1/4 teaspoon dried thyme
- 1/2 teaspoon pepper, divided
- 1/4 cup all-purpose flour
- 2 large egg whites, lightly beaten
- 3/4 cup cornmeal
- 1/4 teaspoon salt
- 2 medium green tomatoes
- 2 medium red tomatoes
- Cooking spray
- 8 slices Canadian bacon, warmed

Directions:
1. Preheat air fryer to 375°. Mix mayonnaise, lime zest and juice, thyme and 1/4 teaspoon pepper; refrigerate until serving. Place flour in a shallow bowl; place egg whites in a separate shallow bowl. In a third bowl, mix cornmeal, salt and remaining 1/4 teaspoon pepper.
2. Cut each tomato crosswise into 4 slices. Lightly coat each slice in flour; shake off excess. Dip in egg whites, then in cornmeal mixture.
3. In batches, place tomatoes on greased tray in air-fryer basket; spritz with cooking spray. Cook until golden brown, 4-6 minutes. Turn; spritz with cooking spray. Cook until golden brown, 4-6 minutes longer.

4. For each serving, stack 1 slice each green tomato, bacon and red tomato. Serve with sauce.

Air Fryer Cauliflower

Servings: 4

Cooking Time: 13 Minutes

Ingredients:

- 1 head cauliflower florets
- 1 tablespoon olive oil
- salt and pepper to taste

Directions:

1. Preheat the air fryer to 390°F.
2. Toss the cauliflower with oil and seasonings in a large bowl.
3. Place in the air fryer basket and cook for 12-13 minutes, shaking the basket halfway through cooking.

Notes

Store leftover cauliflower in an airtight container in the fridge for up to 4-5 days. Reheat in the air fryer or under the broiler until crispy.

Air Fryer Baked Potatoes

Servings: 2

Cooking Time: 40 Minutes

Ingredients:

- 2 medium sized potatoes
- olive oil
- salt
- Optional Toppings:
- Bacon bits
- green onions
- cheese
- sour cream

Directions:

1. Scrub and wash the potatoes and pat dry. Rub with olive oil and pierce all over with a fork. Place into the basket of the air fryer and sprinkle with salt.
2. Cook at 400 degrees for 40 minutes or until fork tender when pierced.

Keto Fried Pickles

Servings: 4

Cooking Time: 7 Minutes

Ingredients:

- 9 large pickles sliced lengthways
- 3/4 + 1 tablespoon almond flour
- 1/2 teaspoon salt
- 1/4 teaspoon pepper
- 1 cup parmesan cheese
- 2 large eggs
- 2 tablespoons sour cream

Directions:

1. Slice your dill pickles lengthways and set aside.
2. In a small bowl, add your almond flour, salt, pepper, and parmesan cheese and mix until combined. In a separate bowl, whisk together the eggs and sour cream.
3. Dip the dill pickles in the wet mixture, followed by the dry mixture. Repeat the process until all the pickles are battered.
4. Add some oil to a non-stick pan. Once hot, add the battered pickles to it and fry for 3-4 minutes, flipping halfway through, until golden brown.
5. Serve the fried pickles immediately with your favorite condiments.

Notes

If you'd like to make this in an air fryer, simply prepare as instructed. Once ready to cook, add them to an air fryer basket and air fry at 200C/400F for 8 minutes.

TO STORE: Leftover pickles should be stored in the refrigerator, covered, for up to three days.

TO FREEZE: Place the cooked and cooled pickles in an airtight container and store them in the freezer for up to two months.

REHEAT: As the fried pickles are 'battered', they should not be microwaved. Instead, reheat them in the air fryer or in a preheated oven.

Cheesy Kale Nests

Servings: 24

Ingredients:

- 8 oz. Tuscan kale (about 1/2 bunch), stemmed, leaves halved lengthwise, then thinly sliced crosswise
- 1 tsp. olive oil
- Kosher salt and pepper
- 2 large eggs
- 1 scallion, finely chopped
- 2 cloves garlic, grated
- 1/2 c. almond flour
- 1 1/2 tbsp. all-purpose flour
- 1/2 tsp. baking powder
- 4 oz. extra-sharp white Cheddar, finely shredded

Directions:

1. Heat air fryer to 400°F. In large bowl, rub kale with oil and 1/2 teaspoon salt. Transfer to air fryer basket and cook until wilted, 1 minute; return to same large bowl and let cool.
2. In medium bowl, whisk together eggs, scallion, and garlic. In small bowl, whisk together both flours and baking powder. Fold egg mixture, flour mixture, and cheese into kale.
3. Line air fryer basket with parchment paper, leaving enough room around edges to allow for air circulation. Working in batches, drop 1-tablespoon spoonfuls of mixture into basket, spacing 1 inch apart. Cook until nests turn golden, about 4 minutes. Using small offset spatula or fork, carefully flip each nest and cook until golden brown and edges are crisp, 1 minute more. Repeat with remaining kale mixture. Serve immediately.

Crispy Air Fryer Lemon Broccoli

Servings: 4

Cooking Time: 8 Minutes

Ingredients:

- 300g broccoli, chopped into florets
- 1 1/2 tbs olive oil
- 1 tsp garlic powder
- 1 lemon, 1 tsp zest
- 1/4 tsp chilli flakes
- 1 pinch black pepper (to taste)

Directions:

1. Place the broccoli florets in a large bowl, add the oil, garlic powder, lemon zest, chilli flakes and black pepper and toss well to coat.
2. Heat the air fryer to 180°C and cook the broccoli for 8 minutes, shaking halfway through.

Air Fryer Vegetarian Pumpkin Schnitzel

Servings: 2

Cooking Time: 30 Minutes

Ingredients:

- 500g potatoes, peeled, cut into 3-4cm pieces
- 250g swede or turnip, peeled, cut into 3-4cm pieces
- 2 1/2 tbsp extra virgin olive oil
- 1/2 cup Panko breadcrumbs
- 1/4 cup finely grated cheddar
- 2 tbsp finely chopped hazelnuts
- 1 tbsp finely chopped flat-leaf parsley, plus extra to serve
- 500g butternut pumpkin, peeled
- 1 egg
- Lemon wedges, to serve
- Select all Ingredients:

Directions:

1. Place potatoes and turnip in a medium saucepan and cover with water. Season with salt. Bring to the boil over high heat. Gently boil, covered, for 15 minutes or until tender. Drain well and return to pan. Add 2 tablespoons oil and mash until smooth. Season with salt and pepper.

2. Meanwhile, Preheat Philips Airfryer to 180C.

3. Combine breadcrumbs, cheddar, hazelnuts, parsley and remaining oil in a shallow dish. Season with salt and pepper. Cut pumpkin into 1cm thick slices. Lightly beat egg on a shallow plate.

4. Dip pumpkin into egg to cover all over. Press into breadcrumb mixture to coat all over. Place in the basket, using the grill separator to arrange a second layer of pumpkin. Insert basket into Airfryer. Cook for 12 minutes or until golden and tender.

5. Serve pumpkin schnitzels with mash and lemon wedges. Sprinkle with extra chopped parsley.

Air Fryer Vegetables

Servings: 4
Cooking Time: 9 Minutes

Ingredients:

- 1 small zucchini sliced
- 2 bell peppers diced
- 1 ½ tablespoon olive oil
- 1 teaspoon Italian seasoning
- 1 garlic clove minced
- salt and pepper to taste

Directions:

1. Preheat air fryer to 380°F.

2. In a large bowl mix vegetables, garlic, seasonings, and oil together until evenly coated.

3. Add to the air fryer basket and cook for 7-9 minutes or until tender-crisp.

Notes

Cut veggies in uniformly and avoid overfilling the air fryer so the veggies evenly cook.

Mexican Street Corn

Servings: 4
Cooking Time: 12 Minutes

Ingredients:

- 4 ears corn, husks and silks removed
- 1 cup Mexican crema
- 2 limes, zested and juiced
- ½ cup cotija cheese, finely crumbled
- ⅓ cup cilantro, finely chopped

- 2 tablespoons chile de arbol powder or other chili powder
- Items Needed:
- Empty squeeze bottle with lid
- Funnel (optional)

Directions:

1. Place the cooking pot into the base of the Smart Indoor Grill, followed by the grill grate.

2. Select the Air Grill function on max heat, adjust time to 12 minutes, press Shake, then press Start/Pause to preheat.

3. Place the corn onto the preheated grill grate, then close the lid.

4. Flip the corn halfway through cooking. The Shake Reminder will let you know when.

5. Place the crema and lime juice in a medium bowl and stir until well combined, then transfer into the squeeze bottle. Place the cap onto the squeeze bottle and then set aside until ready to use.

6. Note: Using a funnel may help transferring the crema to the squeeze bottle. Remove the corn when done and place onto a platter.

7. Use the squeeze bottle to apply the crema to the top of the corn, then sprinkle the lime zest, cotija cheese, cilantro, and chile powder over the top and serve.

Air-fried Buffalo Cauliflower

Servings: 2
Cooking Time: 10 Minutes

Ingredients:

- 1 2.25 pound head cauliflower, trimmed and broken into florets
- ¼ cup bottled cayenne pepper sauce (such as Frank's Red Hot®)
- 2 tablespoon melted butter
- 2 teaspoon vinegar
- ⅛ teaspoon garlic powder
- Kosher salt (optional)
- Thinly sliced green onions (optional)
- Purchased blue cheese dip or salad dressing

Directions:

1. Preheat air fryer to 400° F, according to manufacturer's directions.

2. In a large bowl, combine cauliflower, hot sauce, butter, vinegar, and garlic powder. Transfer half of the cauliflower to the air fryer basket and cook 10 to 12 minutes, shaking the basket every 5 minutes. Keep warm on a baking sheet in a 200°F. oven while frying remaining cauliflower. Sprinkle with kosher salt and green onions before serving, if desired. Serve with blue cheese dip.

Air Fryer Squash

Servings: 4
Cooking Time: 7 Minutes

Ingredients:

- 1 medium summer squash or zucchini
- ½ teaspoon Italian seasoning
- 1 tablespoon olive oil
- salt & pepper to taste

Directions:

1. Slice squash or zucchini into ½" slices.
2. Toss with olive oil and seasonings.
3. Preheat air fryer to 400°F.
4. Add squash and cook 6-7 minutes or until tender crisp. Cook for 2 minutes longer if you prefer a softer squash.

Ginger And Soy Salmon Fillets With Broccoli

Servings: 2

Ingredients:

- Deselect All
- 2 cups small broccoli florets
- 2 tablespoons vegetable oil
- Kosher salt and freshly ground black pepper
- 1 tablespoon soy sauce
- 1 teaspoon light brown sugar
- 1 teaspoon rice vinegar
- 1/4 teaspoon cornstarch
- One 1/2-inch piece ginger, peeled and grated

- 2 skin-on salmon fillets (6 ounces each)
- 1 scallion, thinly sliced
- Cooked white rice, for serving

Directions:

1. Toss the broccoli with 1 tablespoon of the oil in a bowl until coated. Season with salt and pepper. Transfer the broccoli to a 3.5-quart air fryer.

2. Stir together the soy sauce, sugar, vinegar, cornstarch and ginger in a small bowl. Brush the salmon fillets on all sides with the remaining 1 tablespoon oil, then with the sauce. Arrange the salmon flesh-side down on top of the broccoli.

3. Cook at 375 degrees F until the broccoli is tender and the salmon is cooked through, 10 to 12 minutes for medium to well done, depending on the thickness of your fillets. Transfer to serving plates, sprinkle with the scallion slices and serve with rice.

Notes

You can substitute 2 tablespoons store-bought teriyaki sauce for the soy sauce, brown sugar and vinegar. If light brown sugar isn't available, feel free to use dark brown sugar.

Air Fryer Blooming Onion

Servings: 4

Ingredients:

- FOR THE ONION
- 1 large yellow onion
- 3 large eggs
- 1 c. breadcrumbs
- 2 tsp. paprika
- 1 tsp. garlic powder
- 1 tsp. onion powder
- 1 tsp. kosher salt
- 3 tbsp. extra-virgin olive oil
- FOR THE SAUCE
- 2/3 c. mayonnaise
- 2 tbsp. ketchup
- 1 tsp. horseradish
- 1/2 tsp. paprika
- 1/2 tsp. garlic powder

- 1/4 tsp. dried oregano
- Kosher salt

Directions:

1. Slice off onion stem and set onion on flat side. Cut an inch from the root down, into 12 to 16 sections, being careful not to cut all the way through. Flip over and gently pull out sections of onion to separate petals.
2. In a shallow bowl, whisk together eggs and 1 tablespoon water. In another shallow bowl, whisk together breadcrumbs and spices. Dip onion into egg wash, then dredge in breadcrumb mixture, using a spoon to fully coat. Drizzle onion with oil.
3. Place in basket of air fryer and cook at 375° until onion is tender all the way through, 20 to 25 minutes. Drizzle with more oil as desired.
4. Meanwhile make sauce: In a medium bowl, whisk together mayonnaise, ketchup, horseradish, paprika, garlic powder, and dried oregano. Season with salt.
5. Serve onion with sauce, for dipping.

Air Fryer Broccoli And Cauliflower

Servings: 4

Cooking Time: 8 Minutes

Ingredients:

- 2 cups broccoli florets cut into bite size pieces
- 2 cups cauliflower florets cut into bite size pieces
- 2 tablespoons extra virgin olive oil
- 1 teaspoon garlic powder
- 1/2 teaspoon kosher salt

Directions:

1. In a large bowl, add fresh broccoli and fresh cauliflower.
2. Then add in olive oil, garlic powder, and salt, tossing together until vegetables are well coated.
3. Spray olive oil spray into the basket to make sure vegetables get crispier edges and do not stick.
4. Pour vegetables into the air fryer basket. Air fry at 380 degrees F for 8-10 minutes until the vegetables have crisp edges and are golden brown.

5. Toss or shake the basket halfway through the cooking process.
6. Serve while hot.

Notes

Optional Additional Toppings: Fresh lemon juice and zest, sautéed bell peppers, sprinkle of parmesan cheese, lemon zest or creamy cheese sauce.

Cooking Tips: You can cut and season the florets in advance which makes meal prep even easier. Precut florets can be found in the produce section of your local grocery store, just be sure and cut larger pieces so every piece is bite size.

Substitutions: Use refined coconut oil, avocado oil or vegetable oil in place of olive oil.

Air Fryer Roasted Baby Potatoes

Servings: 4

Cooking Time: 15 Minutes

Ingredients:

- 650g baby potatoes, washed, dried and cut into halves
- 3 tbs fresh rosemary, chopped
- 1/2 tsp paprika
- 1 tsp salt
- 1/4 tsp pepper
- 1 tbs garlic powder
- 2 tbs olive oil

Directions:

1. Preheat the air fryer to 200°C.
2. Place the baby potatoes in a medium sized bowl. Sprinkle with rosemary, paprika, salt, pepper, garlic powder, and olive oil. Spread the baby potatoes evenly inside the air fryer basket. Do not overcrowd.
3. Bake in the air fryer for 15 minutes, tossing halfway through the cooking process

Cajun Prawns With Potato & Corn

Servings: 4

Ingredients:

- 500g baby new potatoes
- 1 tbsp olive oil
- 4 corn on the cobs
- 300g king prawns, shell on
- 2 tsp Cajun spice
- 1 tbsp fresh lemon juice
- 2 tbsp unsalted butter
- 2 tsp Worcestershire sauce
- Fresh cracked pepper, to taste
- Flaked sea salt, to taste
- Lemon wedges, for serving
- Optional for serving
- 2 sprigs fresh thyme, leaves picked from stems and roughly chopped
- 4 sprigs parsley, chopped

Directions:

1. Insert crisper paniere in pan and place pan in unit. Preheat unit by selecting AIR FRY, set temperature to 180°C and set time to 3 minutes. Select START/STOP to begin.
2. In a bowl, toss potatoes with oil. In a separate bowl, combine corn, prawns, cajun spice, lemon juice, butter, Worcestershire sauce, pepper and salt. Toss to combine and reserve.
3. Once unit has preheated, remove pan and place potatoes on crisper paniere. Reinsert pan, select AIR FRY, set temperature to 180°C and set time for 20 minutes. Select START/STOP to begin.
4. After 15 minutes, remove pan and add corn and prawn mixture. Shake well to combine, then reinsert pan to resume cooking for an additional 5 minutes.
5. After 20 total minutes, remove pan and place food on panierter. Serve with lemon wedges and fresh herbs, if desired.
6. TIP For even more flavour, pour any leftover butter or juices from cooking over the finished dish.

FAVORITE AIR FRYER RECIPES

Air Fryer Flatbread Pizzas

Servings: 2
Cooking Time: 10 Minutes

Ingredients:

- 2 pre-cooked flatbread or naan
- 1/2 cup (120 ml) pizza sauce or tomato sauce
- 1/3 cup (40 g) shredded cheese
- salt , to taste
- black pepper , to taste
- OPTIONAL TOPPINGS
- Pepperoni, cooked Sausage, Bacon pieces, diced Ham, sliced or diced Tomatoes, Mushrooms, Pineapple, etc.
- OTHER SAUCE OPTIONS
- BBQ Sauce, Salsa, White (Alfredo) Sauce, Pesto, etc.
- EQUIPMENT
- Air Fryer
- Air Fryer Rack optional

Directions:

1. Place the flatbreads (naan) in air fryer bottom side up (make sure it is in just a single layer - cook in batches if needed).
2. Air Fry at 360°F/182°C about 2-3 minutes. Flip the flatbreads over. Continue to Air fry at 360°F/182°C for another 1-2 minutes (if you want the crust extra crispy - air fry each side a couple minutes more).
3. Divide the sauce between the toasted flatbreads. Top with cheese and add additional salt, pepper and other preferred toppings.
4. To keep your topping from flying around, place an air fryer rack over the flatbread pizzas.
5. Air Fry the pizzas at 360°F/182°C for 2-5 minutes or until heated through and cheese is melted.

Air Fryer Cacio E Pepe Spaghetti Squash

Servings: 2

Ingredients:

- 1 medium spaghetti squash (about 2 lb.), halved lengthwise
- 2 tbsp. extra-virgin olive oil, plus more for drizzling
- 2 tbsp. grated Parmesan, plus more for serving
- 3/4 tsp. kosher salt
- 1/2 tsp. freshly ground black pepper, plus more
- Torn fresh basil leaves, torn, for serving

Directions:

1. In an air-fryer basket, arrange one-half of squash cut side down. Cook at 360° until squash is tender and golden, 20 to 25 minutes. Repeat with other half of squash.
2. Scrape and fluff insides of squash with a fork and transfer to a medium bowl; reserve shells for serving, if desired. Add oil, Parmesan, salt, and 1/2 teaspoon pepper to bowl and toss to combine.
3. Stuff insides back into reserved shells or divide between plates. Drizzle with more oil. Top with more Parmesan, pepper, and basil.

Air Fryer Bratwurst

Servings: 5
Cooking Time: 15 Minutes

Ingredients:

- 1 pound uncooked bratwurst
- 5 hoagie rolls optional
- toppings for serving dijon mustard, sauerkraut, pickles, etc

Directions:

1. Preheat the air fryer to 360°F.
2. Place the brats in a single layer in the air fryer basket.
3. Cook them for 8 minutes, then flip and cook for an additional 5-6 minutes or until they reach an internal temperature of 165°F.
4. Serve in rolls and/or with desired toppings.

Notes

Ensure brats reach an internal temperature of 165°F.

Do not pierce the brats before cooking or they will lose their juices. Use caution when checking the temperature, they can squirt hot liquid when pierced.

Allow brats to cool for a few minutes before serving or topping.

Nutrition: al information is for brats only and does not include toppings or buns. Information is an estimate and will vary based on brands.

Store leftovers in an airtight container in the fridge for up to 3 days.

Reheat leftovers in the air fryer for up to 5 minutes or until heated through.

Leftovers are great added to pasta or pizza.

Air Fryer Taco Calzones

Servings: 4
Cooking Time: 10 Minutes

Ingredients:

- 1 tube Pillsbury thin crust pizza dough
- 1 cup taco meat
- 1 cup shredded cheddar

Directions:

1. Spread out your sheet of pizza dough on a clean surface. Using a pizza cutter, cut the dough into 4 even squares.
2. Cut each square into a large circle using the pizza cutter. Set the dough scraps aside to make cinnamon sugar bites.
3. Top one half of each circle of dough with 1/4 cup taco meat and 1/4 cup shredded cheese.
4. Fold the empty half over the meat and cheese and press the edges of the dough together with a fork to seal it tightly. Repeat with all four calzones.
5. Gently pick up each calzone and spray it with pan spray or olive oil. Arrange them in your Air Fryer basket.
6. Cook the calzones at 325° for 8-10 minutes. Watch them closely at the 8 minute mark so you don't overcook them.
7. Serve with salsa and sour cream.
8. To make cinnamon sugar bites, cut the scraps of dough into even sized pieces, about 2 inches long. Add them to the Air Fryer basket and cook at 325° for 5 minutes. Immediately toss with 1:4 cinnamon sugar mixture.

Air Fryer Hot Dogs

Servings: 4

Cooking Time: 8 Minutes

Ingredients:

- 4 hot dogs
- 4 hot dog buns
- Optional toppings: ketchup, relish, mustard, chopped onions

Directions:

1. Heat an air fryer to 375°F.
2. Place 4 hot dogs in a single layer in the air fryer basket. Air fry until the hot dogs look plump and are slightly browned, flipping them halfway through, 5 to 6 minutes total.
3. If you want toasted buns, transfer a hot dog into each bun. Return to the air fryer basket in a single layer and air fry until the buns are toasted, about 2 minutes. Serve with desired toppings.

Air Fryer Tostones

Servings: 2

Cooking Time: 20 Minutes

Ingredients:

- 1 large green plantain (ends trimmed and peeled (6 oz after))
- olive oil spray (I like Bertolli)
- 1 cup water
- 1 teaspoon kosher salt
- 3/4 teaspoon garlic powder

Directions:

1. With a sharp knife cut a slit along the length of the plantain skin, this will make it easier to peel. Cut the plantain into 1 inch pieces, 8 total.
2. In a small bowl combine the water with salt and garlic powder.
3. Preheat the air fryer to 400F.
4. When ready, spritz the plantain with olive oil and cook 6 minutes, you might have to do this in 2 batches.

5. Remove from the air fryer and while they are hot mash them with a tostonera or the bottom of a jar or measuring cup to flatten.
6. Dip them in the seasoned water and set aside.
7. Preheat the air fryer to 400F once again and cook, in batches 5 minutes on each side, spraying both sides of the plantains with olive oil.
8. When done, give them another spritz of oil and season with salt. Eat right away.

Air Fryer Pita Pizzas

Servings: 1

Cooking Time: 10 Minutes

Ingredients:

- 1 pita bread
- 2 Tablespoons (30 ml) pizza sauce or tomato sauce
- 1/4 cup (28 g) shredded cheese
- salt , to taste
- black pepper , to taste
- OPTIONAL TOPPINGS
- Pepperoni, cooked Sausage, Bacon pieces, diced Ham, sliced or diced Tomatoes, Mushrooms, Pineapple, etc.
- OTHER SAUCE OPTIONS
- BBQ Sauce, Salsa, White (Alfredo) Sauce, Pesto, etc.
- EQUIPMENT
- Air Fryer
- Air Fryer Rack optional

Directions:

1. Place the pita in air fryer (if making multiple pita pizzas, make sure it is in just a single layer - cook in batches if needed). Air Fry at 360°F/182°C for 2 minutes.
2. Flip the pita bread over. Continue to Air fry at 360°F/182°C for another 1-2 minutes (if you want the crust extra crispy - air fry each side a couple minutes more).
3. Spread the sauce over the toasted pita bread. Top with cheese and add additional salt, pepper and other preferred toppings.

4. To keep your topping from flying around, place an air fryer rack over the pita pizzas.

5. Air Fry the pizzas at 360°F/182°C for 2-5 minutes or until heated through and cheese is melted. Allow to cool for a couple minutes, then slice and serve warm.

Air Fryer Mini Corn Dogs

Servings: 4
Cooking Time: 8 Minutes

Ingredients:

- 20 mini corn dogs frozen
- toppings Ketchup, mustard

Directions:

1. Place the mini corn dogs into the air fryer basket, without stacking or overlapping. If you have a smaller basket, air fry 10 at a time.

2. Air fry at 380 degrees F for 9-11 minutes, or until corn dogs reach your desired crispness and the hot dog in the middle is cooked.

3. Serve with your favorite toppings.

Notes

I make this recipe in my Cosori 8 qt. air fryer or 6.8 quart air fryer. Depending on your air fryer, size and wattages, cooking time may need to be adjusted 1-2 minutes.

Air Fryer Reheating Leftover Pizza

Servings: 1
Cooking Time: 6 Minutes

Ingredients:

- 1-2 slices leftover pizza
- oil spray , (optional to lightly coat the pizza so toppings don't dry out - need depends on yoout particular toppings)
- EQUIPMENT
- Air Fryer

Directions:

1. Place foil or perforated parchment sheet to base on air fryer basket, rack or tray. Place the pizza on top. If needed, lightly spray the top of pizza so that the toppings don't burn or dry out (optional).

2. Air Fry at 360°F/180°C for 3-6 minutes or until cooked to your desired crispness. If unsure, start cooking for 3 minutes first. Then check to see if it's to your liking. Cook additional minute or two if you want the pizza to be crispier. Deep dish crusts will take a little longer, while thin crust will be slightly quicker.

3. Let the slice of pizza cool for a touch & enjoy!

Notes

Air Frying Tips and Notes:

Recipe timing is based on a non-preheated air fryer. If cooking in multiple slices back to back, the following slices may cook a little quicker because the air fryer is already hot.

Recipes were tested in 3.7 to 6 qt. air fryers. If using a larger air fryer, the pizza slices might cook quicker so adjust cooking time.

Air-fryer White Pizza

Servings: 4
Cooking Time: 6 Minutes

Ingredients:

- 1 recipe Food Processor Pizza Dough
- 2 tablespoon olive oil
- ¾ cup whole milk ricotta cheese
- 1 cup shredded mozzarella cheese (4 oz.)
- 1 teaspoon crushed red pepper
- ½ teaspoon sea salt flakes
- 2 tablespoon chopped fresh basil
- Honey (optional)
- Food Processor Pizza Dough
- Olive oil or nonstick cooking spray
- 2 cup all-purpose flour
- 1 package active dry yeast
- 1 teaspoon sugar
- ½ teaspoon salt
- 1 tablespoon olive oil
- ⅔ cup warm water (105°F to 115°F)

Directions:

1. Preheat air fryer at 375°F. Divide Food Processor Pizza Dough into four 4-oz. portions. On a lightly

floured surface, roll one portion of dough into an 8-inch circle. Prick all over with a fork. Place in air-fryer basket and cook 3 minutes. Remove from basket and place, top side down, on work surface.

2. Drizzle crust lightly with 1 1/2 tsp. of the oil and spread with 3 Tbsp. of the ricotta cheese. Sprinkle with 1/4 cup of the mozzarella cheese, 1/4 tsp. of the crushed red pepper, and 1/8 tsp. of the salt. Return pizza to air-fryer basket and cook 3 to 4 minutes or until cheese is melted and golden. Repeat with remaining dough and toppings.

3. Before serving, sprinkle pizzas with basil and, if desired, drizzle with honey.

4. Food Processor Pizza Dough

5. Coat a medium bowl with nonstick cooking spray; set aside. In a food processor combine flour, yeast, sugar, and salt. With the food processor running, add olive oil and warm water. Process until a dough forms. Remove and shape into a smooth ball. Place dough in the prepared bowl; turn once to coat dough surface. Cover bowl with plastic wrap. Let stand in a warm place until doubled in size (45 to 60 minutes).

6. *Tip

7. For a delicious garlic-herb crust, add 1 Tbsp. dried Italian seasoning, crushed, and 2 cloves garlic, minced, to the flour mixture when preparing the dough.

8. *Make-Ahead Directions:

9. At this point, the dough portions can be placed in a storage container that has been lightly coated with nonstick cooking spray or brushed with olive oil. Cover and store in the refrigerator for up to 24 hours. Or place each dough portion in a freezer bag that has been lightly coated with nonstick cooking spray or brushed with olive oil. Seal, label, and freeze up to 3 months. Thaw in the refrigerator before using.

Air Fryer Spaghetti Squash

Servings: 4

Cooking Time: 35 Minutes

Ingredients:

- 1 medium spaghetti squash about 3 pounds
- 1 tablespoon olive oil
- ½ teaspoon kosher salt
- ¼ teaspoon black pepper

Directions:

1. Preheat the air fryer to 370°F.

2. Cut the spaghetti squash in half lengthwise. Scoop out the seeds and discard (or save for roasting).

3. Brush the cut side of the squash with oil and season with salt & pepper.

4. Place cut side up in the air fryer and cook 25-30 minutes or until tender and the strands separate easily with a fork.

5. Once cooked, run a fork along the strands of the squash to separate.

6. Toss with butter if desired or season with additional salt and pepper.

Notes

Spaghetti squash seeds can be saved and cooked like pumpkin seeds.

Cook time can vary slightly based on the size of the squash.

Once the strands are separated, they can be topped with your favorite meat sauce and placed back into the squash shells. Top them with mozzarella cheese and air fryer until browned and bubbly.

Keep leftovers in the fridge for up to 3 days. Freeze leftovers in zippered bags for up to 6 months. Let thaw at room temperature before using.

Air Fryer Grilled Cheese And Ham Crescent Pockets

Servings: 4

Ingredients:

- 1 can (8 oz) refrigerated Pillsbury™ Original Crescent Rolls (8 Count) or 1 can (8 oz) refrigerated Pillsbury™ Original Crescent Dough Sheet
- 4 slices (0.8 oz each) Swiss cheese, cut in half (from 7-oz package)
- 4 slices (4 oz) cooked deli ham (from 7-oz package)

Directions:

1. Cut two 8-inch rounds of cooking parchment paper. Place round in bottom of air fryer basket. Spray with cooking spray.
2. If using crescent rolls, separate dough into 4 rectangles; reshape each rectangle to form 6x4-inch rectangle, firmly pressing perforations to seal; if using dough sheet, unroll and cut into 4 (6x4-inch) rectangles.
3. Place one cheese slice half on center of each rectangle to within 1/2 inch of edge. Top each with 1 slice ham (folding in half to fit), and top with another cheese slice half. Fold dough from top over cheese and ham; firmly press edges with fork to seal. Place two filled crescents onto parchment round in basket of air fryer, spacing apart.
4. Set air fryer to 325°F; bake 8 to 10 minutes or until deep golden brown on top and sturdy enough to turn over with tongs. With tongs or spatula, carefully turn over crescents, and bake 3 to 6 minutes longer or until dough is deep golden brown and thoroughly cooked. Cover loosely with foil to keep warm while baking second batch. Repeat for remaining filled crescents, and place on remaining parchment round in basket of air fryer. Bake as directed as above.

Air Fryer Nuts And Bolts

Servings: 4

Cooking Time: 25 Minutes

Ingredients:

- 2 cups dried farfalle pasta
- 60ml (1/4 cup) extra virgin olive oil
- 2 tbsp brown sugar
- 2 tsp smoked paprika
- 1 tsp onion powder
- 1/2 tsp garlic powder
- 1/2 tsp chilli powder
- 1 cup pretzels
- 80g (1/2 cup) raw macadamias
- 80g (1/2 cup) raw cashews
- 1 cup Kellog's Nutri-grain cereal
- 1 tsp sea salt
- Select all ingredients

Directions:

1. Cook pasta in a large saucepan of boiling salted water until just tender. Drain well. Transfer to a tray. Pat dry with paper towel. Transfer to a large bowl.
2. Combine oil, sugar, paprika, onion, garlic and chilli powders in a small bowl. Spoon half of the mixture over pasta. Toss to coat.
3. Preheat air fryer on 200C. Place pasta in air fryer basket. Cook for 5 minutes. Shake basket. Cook for a further 5-6 minutes or until golden and crisp. Transfer to a large bowl.
4. Place pretzels and nuts in a bowl. Add remaining spice mixture. Toss to coat. Place in air fryer basket. Cook on 180C for 3 minutes. Shake basket. Cook for a further 2-3 minutes or until golden. Add to pasta, then add cereal. Sprinkle with salt. Toss to combine. Cool completely. Serve.

Air Fryer Pizza

Servings: 2

Ingredients:

- 2 (8-oz.) packages pizza dough
- 1 tbsp. extra virgin olive oil, divided
- 1/3 c. crushed tomatoes
- 1 clove garlic, minced
- 1/2 tsp. oregano
- Kosher salt
- Freshly ground black pepper
- 1/2 (8-oz.) mozzarella ball, cut into ¼" slices
- Basil leaves, for serving

Directions:

1. On a clean, floured surface, gently flatten ball of dough with your hands until about 8" in diameter (or roughly smaller than your air fryer basket). Repeat with second dough ball. Brush both with olive oil and transfer one, oil side up, into the basket of your air fryer.

2. In a medium bowl, stir to combine crushed tomatoes, garlic, and oregano, and season with salt and pepper. Spoon half tomato mixture onto the center of rolled out pizza dough, then spread into an even layer, leaving ½" outer crust bare.

3. Add half the mozzarella slices to pizza. Air fry on 400° for 10 to 12 minutes, or until crust is golden and cheese is melted.

4. Remove first pizza from air fryer basket using 2 pairs of tongs, and garnish with basil leaves. Assemble and cook second pizza, garnish, and serve.

Air Fryer Gnocchi With Pesto Dip

Servings: 8

Cooking Time: 10-30 Minutes

Ingredients:

- 2 x 400g packs fresh gnocchi
- 2 tbsp olive oil
- 160g/5⅔oz mayonnaise
- 3 tsp pesto
- salt and freshly ground black pepper

Directions:

1. Preheat the air fryer to 180C. Toss the gnocchi with the oil in a bowl and season well with salt and pepper. Cook in the air fryer for 20 minutes, turning halfway, until crispy and lightly golden.

2. Meanwhile, mix the mayonnaise and pesto together in a small bowl. Serve alongside the gnocchi with some cocktail sticks to skewer the gnocchi for dipping.

3. Recipe Tips

4. The pesto dip can be changed for all kinds of interesting dipping sauces. Cajun mayo, honey sriracha, smoky BBQ or hot honey mustard are just a few easy throw-together dips for these easy party snacks.

5. You can also cook these in a preheated oven at 200C/180C Fan/Gas 6 for 20 minutes, or until golden-brown all over.

Air Fryer Corn Dogs

Servings: 5

Cooking Time: 9 Minutes

Ingredients:

- 5 Corn Dogs

Directions:

1. How To Make Regular Sized Frozen Corn Dogs in the Air Fryer

2. Preheat Air Fryer to 380 degrees Fahrenheit. Prepare the Air Fryer basket with olive oil cooking spray or parchment paper.

3. Place the corn dogs in Air Fryer Basket.

4. Set the cook time to 9 minutes. After 5 minutes, flip the corn dogs in the Air Fryer Basket and then cook for the remainder of time.

5. Serve with your favorite condiments and side items.

6. How To Make Mini Sized Frozen Corn Dogs in the Air Fryer

7. Preheat Air Fryer to 380 degrees Fahrenheit. Prepare the basket with cooking spray or parchment paper.

8. Place the corn dogs in preheated Air Fryer Basket. Be sure to line them up in a single layer.

9. Set the cooking time to 7 minutes. After 4 minutes, flip the mini corn dogs and cook for the remainder of the time.

10. Serve with your favorite condiments or side items.

Notes

It is best to preheat the Air Fryer before making any of your recipes, including frozen corn dogs.

If you're not preheating the Air Fryer cook time will be different. You won't get the same results and your foods may not be cooked thoroughly through.

Just as you would preheat the oven, you want to preheat the Air Fryer as well so that you can ensure you have fully cooked food and that you are also using the correct cook time.

Air Fryer French Bread Pizzas

Servings: 2

Cooking Time: 10 Minutes

Ingredients:

- 1 French bread loaf
- 1/2 cup (120 ml) pizza sauce or tomato sauce
- 1/3 cup (40 g) shredded cheese
- salt , to taste
- black pepper , to taste
- OPTIONAL TOPPINGS
- Pepperoni, cooked Sausage, Bacon pieces, diced Ham, sliced or diced Tomatoes, Mushrooms, Pineapple, etc.
- OTHER SAUCE OPTIONS
- BBQ Sauce, Salsa, White (Alfredo) Sauce, Pesto, etc.
- EQUIPMENT
- Air Fryer
- Air Fryer Rack optional

Directions:

1. Cut French bread loaf to fit the length of your air fryer. Slice in half lengthwise.

2. Lightly spray both sides for an extra crispy crust. Place in air fryer basket/tray with the bottom (crust) side up (only cook in a single layer - cook the pizzas in batches if needed). Air Fry at 360°F/182°C about 2 minutes.

3. Flip the bread, add sauce & toppings.

4. Cover toppings with an air fryer rack to keep toppings from flying around.

5. Air Fry 360°F/182°C for 2-4 minutes or until heated through and cheese is melted. Try air frying for about 2 minutes first. If you want the top to be crispier, add additional minute or two until the pizza is crispy and cheese is melted.

6. Allow pizza to cool for about 2 minutes. Serve warm.

Air Fryer Fried Brown Rice

Servings: 2

Ingredients:

- 1 large carrot, peeled, trimmed, and chopped into small pieces (about 3/4 c.)
- 2 scallions, thinly sliced, white and green parts separated
- 2 tsp. finely chopped fresh ginger (from a 1" piece)
- 1 tbsp. vegetable oil
- 1/4 tsp. kosher salt
- 2 c. long-grain brown rice
- 1 clove garlic, finely chopped
- 2 1/2 tsp. low-sodium soy sauce
- 2 tsp. toasted sesame oil
- Freshly ground black pepper
- 1 large egg, lightly beaten
- 1/2 c. frozen peas, thawed

Directions:

1. In a 7" nonstick round pan, combine carrot, white scallion parts, ginger, vegetable oil, and salt. In an air-fryer basket, place pan. Cook at 400°, stirring halfway through, until onion and carrot are just tender, about 5 minutes.

2. Remove air-fryer basket and add rice, garlic, soy sauce, sesame oil, and a few grinds of pepper to carrot mixture; stir to combine. Continue to cook at 400° until rice is lightly toasted, about 5 minutes more.

3. Remove air-fryer basket and pour egg over half of rice mixture and peas over other half. Continue to

cook at 400° until egg is just set and peas are warm, about 4 minutes more; stir to combine. Top with green scallion parts.

Buttermilk Ranch Dressing

Servings: 16

Ingredients:

- 1 cup buttermilk
- ⅔ cup mayonnaise (I use low fat)
- ⅔ cup sour cream (I use low fat)
- 1 tablespoon fresh chives chopped
- 1 tablespoon fresh dill chopped
- 1 tablespoon fresh parsley chopped
- ¾ teaspoon garlic powder
- ¾ teaspoon onion powder
- ½ teaspoon salt & pepper (each)

Directions:

1. Mix all ingredients in a bowl.
2. Refrigerate at least 30 minutes before serving.

Notes

Reduce buttermilk to ¾ cup to make ranch dip.
If using dried herbs, use 1 teaspoon of each (instead of 1 tablespoon).
Keeps 1 week in the fridge.

Air Fryer Sausage Rolls

Servings: 12

Cooking Time: 10 Minutes

Ingredients:

- Air Fryer Sausage Rolls
- 3 sausages Note 1
- 3 sheets puff pastry
- 1 tbsp sesame seeds
- 1 eggs

Directions:

1. Air Fryer Sausage Rolls
2. Turn the air fryer on to 180°C/350 F for 15 mins
3. Use a knife and chopping board to remove the casing from the sausages
4. Add egg to a small bowl, pierce yoke and whisk

5. Place a sheet of puff pastry (thawed) onto the chopping board and place 1 off the sausages on top
6. Roll the pastry around the sausage, then use a pastry brush to coat the top of the pastry where the 2 bits of pastry will meet
7. Continue to roll the pastry around the sausage and again brush one side of where the pastry joins with the egg
8. Repeat for each sausage
9. Brush the top of the length of the long rolled sausage with egg
10. Sprinkle the top with sesame seeds
11. Use a knife to cut the excess pastry off each end
12. Then cut the long sausage roll into 4 smaller rolls
13. Spray the Air Fryer Basket with oil (or use baking paper) then place raw sausage rolls into Air Fryer (work in batches)
14. Cook sausage rolls in Air Fryer for 7- 9 mins until pastry is golden and crispy
15. Serve with sauce

Air Fryer Totino's Pizza

Servings: 4

Cooking Time: 6 Minutes

Ingredients:

- 1 Totino's Party Pizza

Directions:

1. Remove the frozen pizza from packaging. Lightly spray the air fryer tray or air fryer basket with an air fryer safe cooking spray.
2. Place pizza in basket. No need to preheat air fryer. Air fry at 400 degrees F for 6-8 minutes, until it has a crispy crust and has reached your desired level of crispiness.
3. Serve while hot.

Notes

I love this brand of frozen pizza because they have options for pizza toppings. I love pepperoni, or triple cheese pizza. Unless the pizza is deep dish, the cooking times should be the same.

Air Fryer Frozen Mozzarella Sticks

Servings: 2

Cooking Time: 6 Minutes

Ingredients:

- 10 frozen mozzarella sticks
- marinara sauce or your favorite dipping sauce

Directions:

1. Preheat the air fryer to 360 degrees.
2. Place the frozen mozzarella sticks in the air fryer cook for 6-8 minutes.
3. Pinch slightly (and carefully since they're hot). They are done when the cheese inside is soft and there is give to the mozzarella stick.
4. Remove them from the air fryer and enjoy with a marinara sauce for dipping.

Air Fryer Chili Cheese Dogs

Servings: 2

Cooking Time: 5 Minutes

Ingredients:

- 2 hot dogs
- 2 sausage rolls
- 1/2 cup canned or homemade chili of choice warmed or at room temperature
- 1/2 cup shredded cheddar cheese*

Directions:

1. Preheat your air fryer to 400 degrees.
2. Place the hot dogs inside the air fryer and cook for 4 minutes, turning halfway through.
3. Remove the hot dogs from the air fryer and place inside sausage rolls. Gently place each one in the air fryer and add half of the cheddar cheese evenly on top of the hot dogs.
4. Add the chili and then top with the remaining cheddar cheese.
5. Turn air fryer to 350 degrees and cook for 1-2 minutes until cheese has melted and chili is warm.
6. Carefully remove the chili cheese dogs from the air fryer and enjoy immediately.

Notes

Mexican cheese can be substituted for cheddar cheese

If cooking hot dogs from frozen:

Place small slits on hot dogs using a knife. Cook on 350 (preheated) for 7-8 minutes until hot dog is heated thoroughly.

SNACKS & APPETIZERS RECIPES

Air Fryer Frozen Crinkle Cut Fries

Servings: 4
Cooking Time: 12 Minutes

Ingredients:

- 1 lb. (454 g) Frozen crinkle cut fries
- salt , to taste
- black pepper , to taste
- EQUIPMENT
- Air Fryer

Directions:

1. Place the frozen crinkle fries in the air fryer basket and spread out evenly. No oil spray is needed for the fries. It's already been deep fried in oil, so that's enough to air fry.
2. Air Fry at 400°F/205°C for 10-14 minutes. Shake and gently stir about halfway through cooking. If cooking larger batches, or if your fries don't cook evenly, try turning them multiple times on following batches.
3. Want the fries crisper? If needed air fry for an additional 1-3 minutes or until crisped to your liking. Season with salt & pepper, if desired.

Notes

Air Frying Tips and Notes:

No Oil Necessary. Cook Frozen - Do not thaw first.

Shake or turn if needed. Don't overcrowd the air fryer basket.

Recipe timing is based on a non-preheated air fryer. If cooking in multiple batches of fries back to back, the following batches may cook a little quicker.

Recipes were tested in 3.7 to 6 qt. air fryers. If using a larger air fryer, the fries might cook quicker so adjust cooking time.

Remember to set a timer to shake/flip/toss as directed in recipe.

Air Fryer Zucchini Chips

Servings: 4
Cooking Time: 12 Minutes

Ingredients:

- 1 medium zucchini cut into ½" coins
- 1 beaten egg
- cooking spray
- Crumb Coating
- ⅔ cup Panko bread crumbs
- ⅔ cup seasoned bread crumbs
- 2 tablespoons Parmesan cheese grated
- 1 teaspoon Italian seasoning

Directions:

1. Preheat air fryer to 375°F.
2. Mix coating ingredients in a bowl.
3. Toss zucchini with egg. Dip zucchini into the coating mixture gently pressing to adhere.
4. Lightly spray zucchini with cooking spray.
5. Place in a single layer in the air fryer basket and cook 6 minutes. Turn zucchini over and air fry 6-8 minutes more or until crisp and zucchini is tender.

Notes

For batches, undercook zucchini by 2 minutes. Once all batches are cooked, place them all in the air fryer together for 3 minutes to heat through.Reheat in the air fryer at 375°F for 3-5 minutes or until heated through.

Air Fryer Frozen French Fries

Servings: 4
Cooking Time: 15 Minutes

Ingredients:

- 1 teaspoon oil
- 250 grams frozen french fries (more or less depending on the size of your air fryer and servings you want)
- 1/4 teaspoon seasoning salt

Directions:

1. Preheat air fryer to 400 degrees for 5 minutes.

2. Meanwhile, toss frozen french fries with seasoning salt.

3. Open the air fryer basket and brush with oil (not totally necessary, but ensures the fries will not stick).

4. Place frozen french fries in air fryer basket in a single layer or as close as possible.

5. Cook at 400 degrees F for 15-20 minutes, checking and stirring every 5 minutes, until crispy.

Air Fryer Green Bean Fries

Servings: 4

Cooking Time: 5 Minutes

Ingredients:

- 1 pound green beans fresh
- 1 cup Parmesan cheese
- 1 cup panko bread crumbs
- 1 Tablespoon garlic powder
- 2 eggs
- 1/2 cup all purpose flour
- 2 Tablespoons Olive oil spray

Directions:

1. Preheat Air Fryer to 390 degrees Fahrenheit (199 degrees Celcius).

2. Snap the ends off the fresh green beans, then place them into a colander to rinse. Place the green beans on a paper towel and pat dry.

3. Coat the green beans in the all purpose flour.

4. Whisk together the eggs in a small bowl.

5. Mix together parmesan cheese, panko breadcrumbs, and garlic powder in a separate bowl.

6. Dip the green beans into the egg mixture, and then dip the green beans into the panko and cheese mixture.

7. Coat the green beans well. Add the green beans to a cooling rack as you work to finish the remainder of the green beans. Spray the coated beans with a light coating of olive oil.

8. Place the coated green beans in the Air Fryer basket and air fry for 5 minutes or until golden brown.

9. Sprinkle with additional parmesan cheese or fresh lemon juice if desired and serve with your favorite dipping sauce.

Notes

Arrange your green beans in a single layer: Spreading your green beans out ensures even cooking through the dish.

Cooking spray: You can use olive oil cooking spray, canola oil spray, or avocado oil spray for this recipe.

Coat the green beans well: Use a bit of the breading mix when coating your green beans. The more breading you have, the crispier your green beans will be.

This recipe was made with a basket-style 5.8 qt Cosori Air Fryer. If you're using a different brand, you may have to adjust your cooking time accordingly.

Air Fryer Pasta Chips

Servings: 6

Cooking Time: 20 Minutes

Ingredients:

- 8 ounces rigatoni pasta or bow tie or penne (I used tortiglioni)
- 1 Tablespoon olive oil
- ¼ cup freshly shredded Parmesan cheese plus extra for garnish if desired
- 1 teaspoon Italian dressing mix or your favorite seasoning mix (or ½ teaspoon oregano and ½ teaspoon garlic powder)
- ¼ teaspoon kosher salt
- ¼ teaspoon freshly ground black pepper
- parsley finely chopped, to garnish, optional

Directions:

1. Cook pasta to al dente according to package directions. Do not overcook. Drain and return to the pot to remove moisture.

2. About 2 minutes before pasta is ready, preheat air fryer to 400°F.

3. Add olive oil, parmesan, and seasoning to the pot of pasta, toss to coat.

4. Add pasta to air fryer basket* and cook for 10-12 minutes**, tossing the basket every 3-4 minutes until they are cooked to desired doneness.
5. Cool for about 3-4 minutes before serving. Garnish with parsley and parmesan if desired. Serve with dip, salsa, or hummus.

Notes

While a single layer is best (meaning you may need to do batches), tossing the basket every 3-4 minutes works to cook them all at once!

The "pasta chips" crisp as they cool. If you'd like them to be a bit more crisp after they've cooled, simply pop them back in the air fryer for another couple of minutes.

Avocado Fries With Lime Dipping Sauce

Servings: 4

Ingredients:

- 8 ounces 2 small avocados, peeled, pitted and cut into 16 wedges
- 1 large egg (lightly beaten)
- 3/4 cup panko breadcrumbs (I used gluten-free)
- 1 1/4 teaspoons lime chili seasoning salt (such as Tajin Classic)
- For the lime dipping sauce
- 1/4 cup 0% Greek Yogurt
- 3 tablespoons light mayonnaise
- 2 teaspoons fresh lime juice
- 1/2 teaspoon lime chili seasoning salt (such as Tajin Classic)
- 1/8 teaspoon kosher salt

Directions:

1. Air Fryer Directions:
2. Preheat the air-fryer 390F degrees.
3. Place egg in a shallow bowl. On another plate, combine panko with 1 teaspoon Tajin.
4. Season avocado wedges with 1/4 teaspoon Tajin. Dip each piece first in egg, and then in panko.

5. Spray both sides with oil then transfer to the air fryer and cook 7 to 8 minutes turning halfway. Serve hot with dipping sauce.
6. Oven Directions:
7. Preheat the oven 425F, follow directions above and bake on a sheet pan until golden and crisp, 10 to 15 minutes.

Air Fryer Cinnamon Sugar Tortilla Chips

Servings: 2

Cooking Time: 6 Minutes

Ingredients:

- 2 flour tortillas 6 inch
- 1/4 cup granulated sugar
- 1 tablespoon unsalted butter melted
- 1 teaspoon ground cinnamon

Directions:

1. In a medium bowl, combine the sugar and cinnamon, stirring together. Set cinnamon sugar mixture aside.
2. Lay tortillas flat, and then brush the top of each tortilla with melted butter.
3. Sprinkle cinnamon sugar over tortillas until well coated. Use a pizza cutter and slice tortillas into triangles.
4. Place them in a single layer into the air fryer basket lined with a sheet of parchment paper.
5. Air fry at 350 degrees F for 6-8 minutes, or until they reach desired crispness. Shake basket halfway through the cooking process.
6. Remove chips and place them on a wire rack to cool and remain crispy.

Notes

Optional Dessert Dips: Fresh fruit salsa, marshmallow cream, melted chocolate, strawberry sauce, caramel cinnamon apple dip or cream cheese fruit dip.

Optional Additional Toppings: Fresh strawberries, vanilla ice cream, whipped cream or chocolate shavings.

Cooking Tips: You will definitely want to make a double batch of these tasty treats. Tortilla pieces can slightly overlap if needed.

Air Fryer Ravioli

Servings: 4-6

Ingredients:

- 2 large eggs
- 2 tbsp. whole milk
- 1 c. Italian bread crumbs
- 1/4 c. grated Parmesan, plus more for serving
- 1/4 tsp. kosher salt
- Freshly ground black pepper
- 1 (20-oz.) package refrigerated ravioli
- Cooking spray
- Pesto or marinara, for serving

Directions:

1. In a shallow bowl, whisk eggs and milk. In another shallow bowl, combine bread crumbs and Parmesan; season with salt and a few grinds of pepper.
2. Working one at a time, dip ravioli into egg mixture, then into bread crumb mixture, pressing to adhere. Dip back into egg mixture. Place on a plate.
3. Lightly coat an air-fryer basket with cooking spray. Working in batches, arrange ravioli in basket, spacing about 1/4" apart; spray with cooking spray. Cook at 400°, flipping halfway through and spraying with cooking spray, until golden and cooked through, about 7 minutes.
4. Arrange ravioli on a platter. Top with more Parmesan. Serve warm with pesto alongside for dipping.

Air Fryer Green Beans

Cooking Time: 8 Minutes

Ingredients:

- 1 lb Green beans (trimmed)
- 6 cloves Garlic (minced)
- 1/2 tsp Sea salt
- 1/4 tsp Black pepper
- 2 tbsp Olive oil
- 1 tbsp Lemon juice

Directions:

1. Preheat the air fryer to 375 degrees F (191 degrees C).
2. In a large bowl, combine all the ingredients.
3. Arrange green beans in the air fryer basket, in a single layer.
4. Cook green beans in the air fryer for 7-10 minutes, until tender. Shake the basket halfway through the cook time.

Air Fryer Seasoned French Fries

Servings: 4

Cooking Time: 15 Minutes

Ingredients:

- 4 Russet Potatoes peeled, cut into strips
- 1 tbsp olive oil
- 2 tsp paprika
- 1 tsp kosher salt
- 1 tsp garlic powder
- 1 tsp onion powder
- 1 tsp red pepper flakes
- 1/2 tsp black pepper
- 1/4 tsp cayenne pepper

Directions:

1. Peel, and rinse the potatoes.
2. Using a mandolin slicer or sharp knife, cut the potatoes into strips about ¼ inch in thickness.
3. In a medium bowl, soak the strips of potato in cold water for about 30 minutes, then drain them, and pat them dry with a paper towel.
4. Pour in the olive oil and seasonings, tossing the fries to coat them.
5. Place the fries in the air fryer basket, in a single layer, and cook at 400 degrees F for 15-20 minutes, until they are crispy. Shake the basket halfway through cooking.

Air Fryer Chickpeas Recipe

Servings: 4

Cooking Time: 13 Minutes

Ingredients:

- 1 14 oz Canned chickpeas
- 1 teaspoon smoked paprika or as needed
- ½ teaspoon onion powder
- ¼ teaspoon Cayenne pepper
- 1 Tablespoon Olive oil

Directions:

1. Preheat the oven at 190C/380F for 3 minutes
2. Open the can of chickpeas, drain in a colander and rinse under a cold running water. Make sure the chickpea is drained completely, alternatively dry in with a kitchen towel or paper.
3. In a bowl, combine the drained chickpeas, smoked paprika, onion powder, cayenne pepper, salt, olive oil and mix to combine
4. Pour the seasoned chickpeas in the air fryer basket and spread it out. Cook for 12 to 15 minutes shaking every 5 minutes or so at 190C/390F or until crispy to your liking. Leave to cool for about 5 minutes and serve. Enjoy!

Notes

Tips

If you like the chickpeas to be soft in the middle then cook it for a lesser time. You can start checking from 10 minutes until the desired texture is achieved.

If time is not of the essence, then you can marinate the chickpeas in the spices for about 10 to 15 minutes before air frying.

While it is tempting to cook the chickpeas at 200C/400F, I would advise against it as it would require shaking more often and might even burn easily too.

Store the chickpea at room temperature

Chickpeas vary in size and that is due to the type of brands you choose, if your legume is on the big side, then you may need to cook it longer than 13 minutes. Start checking from 10 minutes for optimum results.

Do not cook more than 1 can of chickpeas at once in the air fryer to allow for even cooking. Cook in batches if need be.

Air Fryer Tortilla Chips

Servings: 4

Cooking Time: 6 Minutes

Ingredients:

- 4 corn tortillas small
- 1 tablespoon olive oil
- 1/2 tsp salt

Directions:

1. Using a pastry brush, or oil spray, brush or spray a light coating of oil onto the tortilla triangles.
2. Use a pizza cutter or sharp knife and cut the tortillas into triangles.
3. Place tortilla wedges into the air fryer basket, laying them in a single layer, without overlap.
4. Sprinkle tortilla pieces with salt or other seasonings you may wish to use.
5. Working in batches, air fry at 350 degrees Fahrenheit for 7-9 minutes, turning the chips halfway through cooking time. Chips will be golden brown and crispy when done.

Notes

When air frying, remember that the cook time may vary depending on type of air fryer, and size and type of tortilla pieces. If using larger tortillas, cooking time may need to be adjusted by a couple minutes.

Placing the tortilla slices in a single layer helps them to cook evenly and become crispy.

For additional flavors, you can use additional spices and seasonings. A few bolder flavors you can add would be: curry powder ,white cheddar popcorn powder, or a light sprinkle of chili powder.

You can also add a simple boost of flavor by adding garlic powder, cinnamon, a dash of lime juice and then season with salt before air frying.

Air-fryer Cheesy Mozzarella Chips

Servings: 6
Cooking Time: 10 Minutes

Ingredients:

- 2 tbs plain flour
- 2 tsp onion powder
- 1/2 tsp garlic salt
- 1/4 tsp ground paprika
- 3 free range eggs
- 1 1/2 cups panko breadcrumbs
- 550g mozzarella
- 5ml olive oil cooking spray
- 1/2 cup basil pesto (to serve)
- 2 sprigs basil, leaves picked (to serve)

Directions:

1. Combine flour, onion powder, garlic salt and paprika in a shallow bowl. Season with pepper. Whisk eggs in a separate shallow bowl. Place breadcrumbs in a separate shallow bowl.
2. Cut mozzarella block in half crossways. Then cut each in half horizontally to form 4 thin pieces. Cut each piece into 5 sticks. Dip mozzarella sticks in flour mixture to coat. Shake off excess. Working in batches, coat mozzarella sticks in egg mixture then in breadcrumbs. Repeat crumbing process to double crumb. Spray the chips with oil after double crumbing.
3. Preheat air fryer to 200°C for 2 minutes. Working in 2 batches, cook mozzarella sticks in air fryer for 4 minutes or until golden. Stand for 2 minutes, then transfer to a board. Top with basil and serve with pesto.

Air Fryer Beet Chips

Servings: 4
Cooking Time: 30 Minutes

Ingredients:

- 3 beets
- 1 Tablespoon olive oil
- 1 teaspoon Kosher salt
- 1 teaspoon ground black pepper

Directions:

1. Carefully peel the beets and then slice them to your desired thickness using a mandolin. (Careful, these are sharp!)
2. Add the sliced beets into a medium sized mixing bowl and then coat with olive oil, salt, and pepper. Mix until the beets are coated evenly.
3. Add the beet chips in a single layer into the basket of the air fryer. It's ok to overlap the beet chips slightly.
4. Air fry beet chips at 320 degrees Fahrenheit for 30 minutes, carefully flipping the beef chips halfway through the cooking process.
5. Start checking on the chips with 5 minutes remaining and pull the chips early if they are browning fast. (This will depend on the size and thickness of the slices.)
6. Remove the beet chips for the air fryer basket and place them on a wire cooling rack for a few minutes before serving.

Notes

This recipe was made with a 1700 watt basket style 5.8 quart Cosori air fryer. If you are using a different size or different brand of air fryer, you may need to add a minute or two. All air fryers cook a little differently.

Store any leftover beet chips in an airtight container for up to 3 days.

Consider spicing things up by adding a ¼ teaspoon of cayenne pepper, white pepper, or even some red pepper flakes.

Air Fryer Keto Onion Rings Recipe

Servings: 4
Cooking Time: 16 Minutes

Ingredients:

- 1 large Onion (sliced into rings 1/2 inch thick)
- 3 tbsp Wholesome Yum Coconut Flour
- 1/4 tsp Sea salt
- 2 large Eggs
- 2/3 cup Pork rinds (~1.8 oz)
- 3 tbsp Wholesome Yum Blanched Almond Flour
- 1/2 tsp Paprika

- 1/2 tsp Garlic powder

Directions:

1. Arrange 3 small, shallow bowls in a line:
2. Coconut flour and sea salt, stirred together
3. Eggs, beaten
4. Pork rinds, almond flour, paprika, and garlic powder, stirred together
5. Lightly grease 2 air fryer oven racks or an air fryer basket.
6. Dredge an onion ring in coconut flour. Dip it in the egg, shake off the excess, then place in the pork rind mixture. Scoop extra pork rind mixture over it, so that it's coated on all size. Place into the air fryer rack or basket. Repeat with all the onion rings, placing them in a single layer without touching. (You may need to cook them in two batches if you don't have 2 air fryer racks.)
7. Preheat the air fryer or air fryer oven to 400 degrees F for 2 to 3 minutes.
8. For an air fryer oven: Place both racks into the air fryer oven. Bake for about 8 minutes, until the top layer is golden. Switch racks and bake for 8 more minutes, until the top layer is golden again.
9. For a regular air fryer: Only half the onion rings will fit into the basket in a single layer. Place the basket into the air fryer. Bake for 16 minutes, until golden. Remove the onion rings, arrange the next batch of uncooked rings, and repeat.

Air Fryer Apple Chips—an Easy Snack

Ingredients:

- 1 red apple
- 2 tbsp sugar
- 1 tbsp dark brown sugar
- 1 tsp cinnamon
- For a healthier version, try making without the added sugar.

Directions:

1. Thinly slice and core the apple. Using a slicing mandolin is preferred. In a medium bowl, combine sugar and cinnamon. Add apple slices and coat well. Line the air fryer basket with perforated parchment paper to prevent sticking. Spread apple slices evenly inside the basket and air fry at 250°F for 1 hour.

Blistered Snap Peas

Servings: 4

Ingredients:

- 1 lb. snap peas, strings removed
- 2 tbsp. olive oil
- 1/2 to 1 teaspoon gochugaru
- Kosher salt
- 1/2 lemon, plus wedges for serving
- Cilantro, for serving

Directions:

1. Place grill basket on grill and heat grill and basket, covered, on high 10 minutes.
2. In large bowl, toss snap peas with oil, gochugaru, and 1/2 teaspoon salt. Add to grill basket and grill, tossing twice, until charred and just tender, 5 to 8 minutes.
3. Squeeze juice of 1/2 lemon on top and toss to combine. Transfer to shallow bowl or platter and serve with additional wedges and sprinkle with cilantro if desired.
4. AIR FRYER DIRECTIONS:
5. Heat air fryer to 400°F. In large bowl, toss snap peas with oil, gochugaru and 1/2 teaspoon salt. Add snap peas to air-fryer basket and air-fry until slightly charred and just tender, 5 to 6 minutes. Squeeze juice of lemon half on top. Using tongs, quickly toss to combine, then transfer snap peas to shallow bowl or platter. Serve with lemon wedges and sprinkle with cilantro.

Frozen Waffle Fries In The Air Fryer

Servings: 4

Cooking Time: 8 Minutes

Ingredients:

- 1 pound frozen waffle fries (1/2 bag)
- OPTIONAL
- Dipping sauce of choice

Directions:

1. Preheat your air fryer to 400 degrees F.
2. Place a single layer of frozen waffle fries in your air fryer. They can overlap slightly.
3. Cook the fries for 8 to 10 minutes, carefully shaking the basket halfway through cooking.
4. Remove the waffle fries from the air fryer, serve with your favorite dipping sauce, and enjoy!

Notes

HOW TO REHEAT WAFFLE FRIES IN THE AIR FRYER:

Preheat your air fryer to 350 degrees.

Place your leftover waffle fries in the air fryer and cook for about 2 minutes, until warmed thoroughly.

Air Fryer Spicy Onion Rings

Servings: 4

Cooking Time: 10 Minutes

Ingredients:

- 2 large sweet onions, sliced 1/2 inch thick
- Batter:
- ⅔ cup buttermilk
- 1 egg
- ¼ cup all-purpose flour
- 1 teaspoon RedHot Chile and Lime Seasoning Blend (such as Frank's®)
- ½ teaspoon adobo all-purpose seasoning (such as Goya®)
- Breading:
- 2 cups panko bread crumbs
- 1 teaspoon adobo all-purpose seasoning (such as Goya®)
- ½ teaspoon RedHot Chile and Lime Seasoning Blend (such as Frank's®)
- olive oil cooking spray
- 1 teaspoon kosher salt, or to taste

Directions:

1. Whisk together buttermilk, egg, flour, chile and lime seasoning, and adobo seasoning for the batter in a shallow bowl. Cover and refrigerate for 30 minutes.
2. Combine panko, adobo seasoning, and chile and lime seasoning in a shallow dish; mix well. Remove batter from the fridge. Dip onion rings first into the batter, then into bread crumb mixture, turning to coat, and gently shake off excess crumbs. Lightly spritz the onion rings with cooking spray on both sides.
3. Preheat the air fryer to 340 degrees F (170 degrees C). Line the air fryer basket with a parchment liner or lightly spray with oil.
4. Place the breaded onion rings into the fryer basket in an even layer, leaving about 1/2-inch space between the slices.
5. Cook until crisp and lightly browned, flipping halfway through, 10 to 12 minutes. You may have to cook in batches, and cooking time may vary depending on the size and brand of your air fryer.
6. Remove from the air fryer, transfer to a baking sheet, sprinkle with kosher salt, and place in a 250 degrees F (120 degrees C) oven to keep warm.
7. Cook's Notes:
8. You can find Chile n' Lime seasoning and Adobo seasoning in the Hispanic section of your supermarket. Adobo should be available at most stores, but if Chile n' Lime is not, use all Adobo.
9. Chilling the batter will make the breading adhere better. You may bread the onion rings, cover early in the day, and refrigerate until ready to cook.

Air Fryer Frozen Tater Tots

Servings: 4
Cooking Time: 14 Minutes

Ingredients:

- 16 ounces tater tots frozen
- seasoning salt to taste

Directions:

1. Preheat air fryer to 400°F.
2. Place tater tots in the air fryer basket in a single layer.
3. Cook for 12-14 minutes shaking the basket halfway through the cooking time.
4. Season with salt to taste and serve.

Notes

Reheat tater tots in the air fryer at the same temperature for only a few minutes.

Air Fryer Tater Tots

Servings: 6-8
Cooking Time: 10-12 Minutes

Ingredients:

- 1 (28 to 32-ounce) package frozen tater tots, divided
- 1/2 teaspoon seasoned salt, such as Lawry's (optional)

Directions:

1. Heat an air fryer to 400°F. Place about 1/2 bag frozen tater tots in a single layer in the basket (they can be touching). Air fry for 6 minutes. Shake the basket to toss the tater tots. Air fry until golden brown and crispy, 4 to 6 minutes more. Transfer to a serving bowl and repeat air frying the remaining tater tots. Sprinkle with 1/4 teaspoon seasoned salt if desired and toss to combine.

Recipe Notes

Storage: Leftovers can be refrigerated in an airtight container for up to 4 days.

Air Fryer Sweet Potato Cubes

Servings: 3
Cooking Time: 10 Minutes

Ingredients:

- 1 large sweet potato, or two medium ones
- 1 tablespoon olive oil
- 1 teaspoon brown sugar (optional)
- ½ teaspoon salt
- ½ teaspoon dried parsley
- Fresh parsley for garnish (optional)

Directions:

1. Preheat your air fryer to 400F.
2. Peel and slice the sweet potato into ½ inch cubes, you should have 2-2 ½ cups sweet potato cubes.
3. Place sweet potato cubes into a large mixing bowl, drizzle with oil and sprinkle seasonings, then toss to combine.
4. Add the seasoned sweet potato to the air fryer, then cook for 8-10 minutes, shaking the basket halfway through.
5. Sprinkle parsley and serve warm.

Air Fryer Curly Fries

Servings: 4
Cooking Time: 10 Minutes

Ingredients:

- 16 ounces frozen curly fries
- ½ teaspoon seasoned salt

Directions:

1. Preheat the air fryer to 400°F.
2. Place the frozen fries in the air fryer basket in a single layer.
3. Cook for 9-10 minutes or until golden brown and crispy.
4. Season with salt and serve.

Printed in Great Britain
by Amazon

33290013R00064